P9-ASD-878

URUGUAY

Uruguay

A Contemporary Survey

Marvin Alisky

FREDERICK A. PRAEGER, *Publishers*
New York · Washington · London

FREDERICK A. PRAEGER, PUBLISHERS
111 Fourth Avenue, New York, N. Y. 10003, U.S.A.
5, Cromwell Place, London S.W. 7, England

Published in the United States of America in 1969
by Frederick A. Praeger, Inc., Publishers

© 1969 by Frederick A. Praeger, Inc.

Library of Congress Catalog Card Number: 76–75236

Printed in the United States of America

Preface

Space does not permit my thanking all of the Uruguayans who helped during my 1967 field trip or, in recent years, in sending me reference material. However, I must single out Juan Felipe Yriart, who in January, 1969, ended his tenure as Uruguayan ambassador to the United States to become director for Latin America of the Food and Agriculture Organization of the United Nations. Sr. Yriart's prompt replies to all inquiries about Uruguayan public life set a standard of service few diplomats in the world can equal.

In Montevideo, Carlos Manini Ríos, first as minister of culture and later as publisher of the daily *La Mañana*, was especially helpful in directing me to pivotal administrators in government and key sources at the National Library needed in this study. The veteran editor of *El Día*, now an educator, Hugo Fernández Artucio and his son Hugo, Jr., were walking encyclopedias of recent Uruguayan history.

In the U.S. Embassy in Montevideo, an old friend, Joe Livornese, counselor of the Embassy, and Nicholas McCausland, political officer, efficiently located labor-management statistics that even some Uruguayan economists had previously sought in vain.

Two U.S. scholars graciously encouraged my efforts to update their earlier studies of Uruguay. Professor Russell H. Fitzgibbon of the University of California at Santa Barbara and Professor Philip B. Taylor, Jr., of the University of Houston, in 1954 and 1960, respectively, wrote excellent books on Uruguay that inspired me to watch the public affairs of that nation closely. Professor L. Vincent Padgett of San Diego State College also supplied valuable reference material.

Any errors in analysis are, of course, my own.

MARVIN ALISKY

Arizona State University
Tempe, Arizona
January, 1969

71-409-

Contents

A section of photographs follows page 88.

URUGUAY

I

The Setting: Land and Resources

GEOGRAPHY

In contrast to the other nations of Latin America, Uruguay has no wasteland—no untilled, isolated regions cut off from its coastlines and capital city. More than 90 per cent of its land area is put to productive use for grazing and to a lesser extent for farming and fishing. No mountains, deserts, or jungles interrupt the smooth topography of its rolling plains. No torturous terrain hinders internal land travel over its good roads, which connect the capital with every other town of consequence within its national borders.

South of the Amazon Basin of Brazil, the green continent of South America swings inward from the Atlantic Ocean, spilling its inland waters into the great river system of the Paraná-Paraguay and the Uruguay. Winding southward for more than 1,000 miles, these brown and gray-green rivers drain half a continent, rushing to merge into the Río de la Plata.

On the eastern bank (Banda Oriental) of the Plata, the Republic of Uruguay neatly spans five degrees of latitude on the map. The only Latin American nation entirely within the temperate zone, Uruguay enjoys mild winters and sunny summers, which make its miles of sandy beaches, from March to November, a major tourist lure for South Americans.

When compared to its giant neighbors, Brazil and Argentina, Uruguay's 72,172 square miles seem very few. But, compared

3

with many leading European nations, Uruguay seems much larger, having more area than England and almost as much as England and Scotland combined. If the United States becomes our measuring standard, Uruguay covers more ground than all the New England states.

The republic's eastern and southern boundaries are the Atlantic Ocean and Río de la Plata coastlines; in the west, the Uruguay River marks its border with Argentina, and the Cuareim River divides it from Brazil in the north. Extending from northeast to southwest, across the nation, the Río Negro is backed up by Uruguay's two big hydroelectric dams to form a lake.

Several minor streams descend in the central and northern regions from foothills with rocks breaking through their wide ridges of surface soil. Only two peaks in the entire country rise more than 2,000 feet above sea level, whereas the coastal plains resemble the flat Argentine pampa. However, the Uruguayan rolling plains, or *campo,* do not possess the same chemical ingredients as do their counterparts on the western side of the Plata. Hence, whereas Argentine soil naturally nurtures alfalfa, Uruguayan soil more easily grows grass. Argentina's pampa more readily lends itself to the grazing of cattle, whereas Uruguay's *campo* more naturally grazes sheep. Wool has, therefore, long been the chief Uruguayan export. Some experimentation with increasing cattle pasture lands has been undertaken successfully, but most Uruguayan cattle still are raised on the grasses indigenous to the Banda Oriental.

FLORA AND FAUNA

Although the treeless pampa has become a stereotype of the Uruguayan terrain, one-third of the land area of the republic does contain some trees, including eucalyptus, willows, poplars, acacias, the soft and fluffy *ombú,* and the scarlet-flowered *ceibo.* A moderate amount of wood gets converted into lumber and fence posts.

Most of the wild animals native to this land have long since become extinct. Hunters still find deer and foxes and the South

American water hog, the *carpincho*. A small armadillo, the *mulita*, also roams the northern foothills. Among the native animals, the fur-bearing nutria stands out in terms of commercial value.

Uruguay's other sought-after animals, the seals, congregate off the Isla de Lobos, an island near Punta del Este, and South America's best preserve of seals. More than 30,000 seals breed there each season, giving the leather and furrier industries of Montevideo an excellent source of supply. The well-organized hide exporters, whose mainstays are sheepskin and cowhide, also handle sealskin.

When the Spaniards came to Uruguay in the sixteenth century, the South American ostrich, the rhea, roamed the Uruguayan flatland, but today it can be found principally on the Argentine pampa, hundreds of miles to the west. Still surviving on the Uruguayan pampa are partridges, and two distinctive native birds, the *terutero* and the *chajá*. Especially interesting to tourists and naturalists, the Uruguayan oven-bird, called the *hornero*, builds its oven-shaped nests of mud on fenceposts and telegraph poles, not only near marshes and plains, but all over the republic. In the south, burrowing owls can be found, as well as the *avestruz*, a type of ostrich similar to the Argentine rhea, whose tail feathers wind up as feather dusters in the homes of Montevideo.

Among the wild fowl, the *pato real*, or royal duck, is the largest, but hunters do not find any of the wild birds numerous. Fishermen do much better, for the rivers of Uruguay contain the *dorado*, the golden salmon, which average about thirty pounds and can weigh up to sixty, even in the Salto Grande Falls of the Uruguay River in the northwestern sector of the republic. Sports fishermen usually head for the Atlantic coastline, where pompano, salmon, and the *corvina* rank as choice game fish. Farther from shore, heavy tackle might reel in finny dynamite, ten-foot sharks, or sixty-five- or seventy-pound rays.

Many Uruguayan inland waters abound in *pejerrey*, but this fish can be caught only in the winter months (June, July, and August in the Southern Hemisphere). During the summer season, river and lake fishermen reel in the *pacú,* the *tararira,* and the *surubí,* remote cousins of North American perch and bass.

The Santa Lucía River flows into the Plata estuary near Montevideo, giving the national capital its best source of fresh water. Farther upstream, the Santa Lucía harbors the best supply of *criolla,* a fish prized by Uruguayans and tourists alike. The possibility of a *criolla* tipping the scales at seventy pounds lures fishermen from Argentina, Brazil, and Chile, as well as some sportsmen all the way from Canada, the United States, and Europe.

Commercially, Uruguay harvests the sea, with fishing fleets from the southern Brazilian waters to the Plata. State-owned trawlers and a factory that cans fish, fish oil, and fish meal are operated by *Servicio Oceanográfico y de Pesca* (SOYP), the Oceanographic and Fishing Service. SOYP supplies Montevideo with much of its seafood and also operates the sealing industry on the Isla de Lobos.

Cattle and Sheep

Neither cattle nor sheep were native to this fertile land when, in 1603, a Spanish conquistador, Hernando Arias, shipped cattle and horses into the deserted pastures of the Banda Oriental. Left to themselves, these wild herds multiplied, so that by the time Montevideo was founded, in 1726, 25 million head of cattle roamed the Uruguayan back country. As Spaniards became Uruguayans, the presence of numerous cattle and horses ensured the evolution of the gaucho, that hard-riding cowboy with soft boots. With cattle always nearby, a gaucho had merely to toss his *boleadoras*—a lasso made by knotting three ropes together and putting stone weights on the free ends, to twine around the animal's legs—and, a few minutes later, meat and leather were assured.

Unfenced ranges emphasized a lonely culture and an independent spirit in the *campo,* which later reflected itself in the political life of the nation. Wire fences and modern ranching methods have relegated gaucho life to carnival time and special celebrations, but the dietary emphasis on beef persists today.

Despite Uruguay's excellent fishing facilities, fish have never eclipsed meat as the mainstay of the dinner table. Uruguayan consumption of meat per inhabitant, 290 pounds a year, remains the highest in the world.

Over the centuries, Spanish cattle strains gave way to English and North American lines, and today beef cattle are mainly Herefords. At first, cattle far outnumbered sheep, for, in the sixteenth century, ranchers from the Canary Islands and Galicia brought in 200 cattle for every 100 sheep, under an agreement with the Council of the Indies. By the late nineteenth century, Uruguayan stockmen had adjusted to the fact that their soil naturally sprouted grasses better suited to grazing sheep than cattle.

AGRICULTURE

When Spaniards in the 1520's fought the Charrúas for a foothold in Uruguay, they discovered that these Indians grew corn, beans, and melons, although hunting for wild game provided a major portion of the food supply. The colonial gaucho made beef and mutton his dietary mainstay. On the eve of national independence from Spain and Portugal, Uruguay welcomed a British merchant named John Mawe. In 1806, Mawe reported that agricultural enterprise remained scanty, with cornfields, or even vegetable gardens, a rare sight.

Throughout the nineteenth century, turbulent political strife reinforced the status quo of an economy based on livestock-raising. But, early in this century, production began to increase for cereal crops—wheat, corn, oats, barley, rice, linseed, and sunflower seed. In recent decades, fruit production has been extensive enough to satisfy the national domestic market with oranges, apples, pears, grapes, and peaches. Principal farming areas are the southern departments of Soriano, Colonia, San José, and Canelones. In 1967, 75 per cent of the land area of the republic was being utilized to graze sheep, cattle, and other livestock, and 15 per cent was being cultivated for crops.

MINERAL RESOURCES

Although not a major mining nation like Bolivia, Peru, or Mexico, Uruguay does possess some iron ore and manganese, but not enough to encourage domestic industry to utilize these mineral resources. Enough marble is quarried annually for the needs of the nation, plus a small surplus for export to Argentina. Granite, sand, and limestone are extracted in sufficient amounts to supply Uruguayan needs. A small amount of agates and onyx are mined, in Salto Department in the northwestern part of the nation, and modest deposits of copper and lead center in Rivera Department in the north-central region. In southeastern Uruguay, the city of Minas was named in colonial times appropriately enough, for today it remains a mining center for granite, slate, and marble quarries. Uruguay's only operating coal mine lies not far from Minas.

DEPARTMENTS

Politically, the republic has a centralized government. For administrative purposes the national territory is divided into provincial units called departments. The nineteen departments of the republic are:

Department	Area (in square miles)
Artigas	4,392
Canelones	1,834
Cerro Largo	5,763
Colonia	2,193
Durazno	5,526
Flores	1,744
Florida	4,674
Lavalleja	4,819
Maldonado	1,586
Montevideo	256
Paysandú	5,115
Río Negro	3,270
Rivera	3,794
Rocha	4,280
Salto	4,865

Department	Area *(in square miles)*
San José	2,688
Soriano	3,560
Tacuarembó	8,112
Treinta y Tres	3,682

In fourteen departments, the capital city has the same name as its department. In the other five, the capital has a different name. These are: Melo for Cerro Largo, Trinidad for Flores, Minas for Lavalleja, Fray Bentos for Río Negro, and Mercedes for Soriano. The capital of the department is usually its major city, with some exceptions, such as Punta del Este, which is in Maldonado Department but is not its capital.

POPULATION DISTRIBUTION

With a population of 2.7 million (estimated at the beginning of 1968), few internal barriers to extensive land utilization, and an annual population increase of 1.3 per cent, Uruguayans are insured decades of continuing wide-open spaces. Eight of ten Uruguayans live in cities, and half of the nation's citizens live in the greater Montevideo metropolitan area. More than 75 per cent of the nation's population resides in the coastal regions, the northern areas being sparsely settled.

Cities and Towns

The 1963 Census counted 1,154,465 inhabitants within the city limits of Montevideo, and a 1967 estimate listed 1.35 million as living in its metropolitan area. The second and third largest cities, Salto and Paysandú, with populations estimated in 1967 at 59,000 and 57,000, have each less than 5 per cent of the Montevideo population.

Montevideo's oldest area, dating from its early colonial days, consists of gray customs warehouses fronting narrow streets that end at the docks of the port. Shipping firms, banks, the stock exchange, the navy's headquarters, and export-import offices form a triangular business area of twenty short blocks narrowing to an apex of the House of Government, which holds the presidential offices, and the Victoria Plaza Hotel, facing each other at the Plaza de Independencia. From the docks to this plaza, from the seawall to the skyscraper Palacio Salvo office building, the Old City peninsula juts into the harbor. Running from the Plaza de Independencia eastward to the suburbs is Montevideo's main street, Avenida 18 de Julio. The "18th of July" commemorates the date in 1830 when Uruguay's first constitution came into force. Large department stores and motion picture theaters line this avenue.

Four blocks east of the Plaza de Independencia the wide Agraciada Avenue begins, cutting a northeastern diagonal across the city. Fifteen blocks north of the 18 de Julio thoroughfare on Agraciada the Legislative Palace dominates a knoll. Inaugurated in 1925 and designed by the distinguished Italian architect Gaetano Moretti, this capitol combines forty-five varieties of marble into mosaic floors and walls. Stained-glass windows depicting historic events in Uruguay make this building an attraction for foreign and domestic tourists alike. Architecturally, the contrast between the austere two-story Government House for the president and the ornate Legislative Palace for the General Assembly attests to the Uruguayan tradition of having the legislative branch of government vigorously counterbalance the executive branch, a political rarity in Latin America.

Twelve blocks east of its beginning, 18 de Julio Avenue forks, its southern branch becoming España Boulevard, running southeast until it ends at the suburban beach of Pocitos. At the fork, the twelve-story Municipal Building of Montevideo faces a large statue of a pioneer gaucho. Eight blocks northeast of this fork, 18 de Julio crosses the main buildings of the national University of the Republic. Nine blocks farther to the northeast, 18 de Julio again forks, its northern branch, 8 de Octubre, heading for the highway to Canelones, a provincial city thirty-two miles northward. Its southern branch, Italia Avenue, passes Batlle Park, containing the national soccer stadium and Clínicas, largest hospital in the nation.

Loosely paralleling Italia is the oceanfront drive, the Rambla, a dozen blocks to the south. The Rambla winds around the beaches of Pocitos, Buceo, and Malvín. Where Bolivia Avenue, running southeast, bisects the Rambla, the upper-income beach suburb of Carrasco begins. Its most prominent landmark is the Hotel Casino Carrasco, scene of roulette gambling during the summer season. To the northeast, beyond the residential mansions and an adjacent industrial park, lies Carrasco International Airport. Eastward stretches the coastal highway to the resort city of Punta del Este.

Like Montevideo, Uruguay's second largest city, Salto, has drawn many Italians and Uruguayans of Italian descent. On the Argentine side of the Uruguay River, Salto's neighboring city of Concordia also has many residents of Italian origin, giving these Argentine and Uruguayan river settlers a friendly cultural bond. Salto's eastern suburbs contain topaz and amethyst mines, but the city's attention faces westward to the river. Its docks and warehouses are modern; its river-front parks and amphitheaters are symbols of civic pride.

The port city of Paysandú on the Uruguay River, named for an eighteenth-century missionary, Father Sandú, receives ocean-going vessels at its docks. North of the city, at Hervidero, the Uruguay narrows, allowing only smaller ships to navigate the seventy miles northward to Salto. The Paysandú Fishing Club lures sportsmen from all over the republic and from various other South American republics, eager to catch the *dorado*. But, basically, the city of Paysandú cannot compete with the beaches of the southeastern coast for tourists, remaining instead a commercial and industrial center for the west-central portion of the nation. Meat, hides, wool, and fish go from its docks, railroad yards, truck depots, and airport to Montevideo and on to foreign nations. A branch of the government meat-packing company, Frigorífico Nacional, has become one of Paysandú's important payrolls.

North of the department of Salto lies the department of Artigas, occupying the northwestern corner of the republic. Its important crops are oranges, grapes, and sugar cane. This sparsely settled department has only 55,000 people, half of them living in the capital city of Artigas, ninety miles east of the Uruguay River, on the Cuareim River, marking the border between Uruguay and Brazil. The only other important city of the department, Bella Unión, on the Uruguay River, faces the Argentine town of Monte Caseros. Bella Unión also has a road running near the juncture of the Uruguay and Cuareim rivers, into Brazil.

The city of Rivera, midway on the northern border of the nation betwen Bella Unión and the Atlantic seaboard, faces the Brazilian city of Livramento. No fence or river or traditional boundary-line barriers separate these two cities. One crosses one of the main streets from Rivera into Livramento, from Uruguay into Brazil, with only a tiny marker reminding him of the international location. As a consequence, Rivera has become the Uruguayan gateway for smugglers taking contraband into the republic from Brazil.

To the southeast, the border crossing from Chuy in Uruguay to Chuí in Brazil has a more formal customs and immigration setup. Chuy is in the department of Rocha, which forms part of the eastern and part of the southern boundary of Uruguay, facing the Atlantic Ocean. Along the coast, an excellent paved highway connects miles and miles of beach resorts, running from Santa Teresa Fortress and National Park southwestward to Punta del Este, which is located in the neighboring department of Maldonado.

The International Fishing Bureau in Paris officially lists the southeastern coast of Uruguay, from Piriápolis to Punta del Este as the fifth largest fishing ground in the world. Along this coastal fringe, fifty to sixty miles wide, the salinity content of the water remains at just the correct level to permit both sea and river species of fish—in all, more than sixty varieties—to live side by side.

Only seventy miles east of Montevideo, the peninsula of Punta del Este should really have been named Punta del Sur, for it represents Uruguay's southernmost point, not its easternmost point. With a winter climate similar to that of Cannes, Nice, or Biarritz on the French Riviera, Punta del Este is the most important city on the Uruguayan Riviera. Luxury hotels, gambling casinos, deluxe restaurants, plus many moderately priced hotels and eating establishments for middle-class visitors make Punta del Este the tourist capital of Uruguay. Country clubs, golf courses, and the marinas of deep-sea fishing make Punta del Este not only Uruguay's adult playground, but that of Argentina and southern Brazil as well. Punta del Este has hosted such historic gatherings as the signing of the charter of the Alliance for Progress in August, 1961, and the meeting of the presidents of the Western Hemisphere republics under the auspices of the Organization of American States (OAS) in April, 1967.

Between Punta del Este and Montevideo to the west lie Piriápolis and Atlántida, cities second only to Punta del Este as resort centers. Westward from Montevideo, along a coastline that gradually becomes less an ocean front and more a river front, lies the historic town of Colonia, 120 miles from the national capital. Founded by the Portuguese in 1680, Colonia de Sacramento remains the most colonial settlement in Uruguay. Cobblestone streets lead to the *Casa del Virrey,* containing furniture from the days when Uruguay was the Eastern Bank of the Uruguay River of the Viceroyalty of La Plata, under the king's deputy sitting in Buenos Aires.

Northwest of Colonia, on the Uruguay River, the city of Fray Bentos, capital of the department of Río Negro, has only 18,000 population but hums with a commercial tempo, a packinghouse community with busy slaughterhouses serving the cattle industry.

More than 250 miles of ocean and river coastline possess some of the world's best natural beaches. And, though fishing and swimming are popular, Uruguayans generally have not gone down to the sea in ships. Commercially, only 5 per cent of Uruguay's total exports leave its shores in merchant ships flying the Uruguayan flag.

II

From Buffer State to Functioning Democracy

DISCOVERY

Juan Díaz de Solís, Spanish explorer and conqueror, sailed southward along the eastern coastline of South America in 1516, seeking a strait leading to the other side of this New World. He was the first European to land in Uruguay, seventy miles east of present-day Montevideo.

When Solís got his landing party on the beach, they were suddenly attacked by the Charrúas, the Uruguayan Indians. Even the Charrúas, centuries before, had arrived in empty Uruguay from elsewhere, from Paraguay to the north, where they had been pressured by the larger forces of the Guaraní Indians. The word "Uruguay" itself came from the Guaraní word *uruguä,* which was the Indian name for Río Uruguay, meaning "river where the birds come from." By the end of a bloody afternoon all members of the 1516 landing party had been killed, except the cabin boy. On board the ship, Sebastian Cabot, second in command to Solís, watched horrified. With no reserves for combat, Cabot ordered his skeleton crew to sail back to Spain.

In 1527, Cabot returned with enough Spaniards to secure a base. Thus, eleven years after his capture, the cabin boy was rescued and became the chief interpreter of the Charrúa language and way of life. Cabot built a sturdy fort near the shore. Half a century later that fort became the town of Salvador, the first permanent colonial settlement, but today merely a site for a historical plaque mounted on the stones of a crumbled wall.

Only four years after Solís brought the first Spaniards to the eastern bank of the Uruguay River, the Portuguese came. Captain Ferdinand Magellan, whose crew would go on to become the first men to circumnavigate the globe, sailed cautiously up the Plata a few miles from the southernmost coast of Uruguay. A sailor posted as lookout saw the hill that today Montevideans call the Cerro and reportedly called out *Monte vide eu*—"I see a mountain." Thus, folklore explains the name Montevideo through the Magellan landing.

COLONIAL CONFLICTS

Mexico lured thousands of Spanish adventurers with the gold and glitter of the Aztec Empire. With the Inca realm as its foundation, Peru also became a major possession of the New World empire of Spain. But the Plata region, devoid of wealthy Indian domains, did not beckon the conquerors. From the archaeologists we receive ample evidence that the Plata region, like North America, had few Indians, and none of the obvious wealth of the sixteenth century, the gold and silver amassed by Aztec and Inca princes. Uruguay—and Argentina across the estuary—had the temperate climate that can nurture wheat and graze livestock, but Spaniards intent on plunder for the royal treasury and converts for the Church could not bother much with the scant populace of the flatlands of the Plata area.

From the days of Cabot and Magellan in the 1520's to the coming of the British in 1807 and the independence from Spain soon thereafter, Uruguay remained on the rim of empire, a political and economic backwater whose excellent natural harbors fell victim to the rigidity of Spanish rulers, languishing until the nineteenth century to function as they should and could.

Panama possessed a strategic vantage point from which Spain might attempt to sustain New World trade monopolies for a while, but once British pirates began to roam the Caribbean and South Atlantic, Spanish reluctance to end the Panamanian port monopoly for all goods going to or from the Plata region lost its earlier *raison d'être*. Yet lobbyists whose Panamanian port holdings underwrote their fortunes tabled the pleas from Plata leaders decade after decade.

An uneasy union of the two Iberian powers, from 1580 to 1640, brought the Spanish and Portuguese empires under one ruler. Once Portugal again became free of the Spanish monarchy, however, rivalry intensified. The buffer territory of the eastern bank of the Uruguay River—the *Banda Oriental del Río Uruguay*—served as a natural arena of conflict. Only a corporal's guard of the many overseas regiments actually clashed, but out of that confrontation a political epic unfolded.

After the Spanish founded, abandoned, and refounded Buenos Aires, the Portuguese countered by establishing, in 1680, directly across the Plata from Buenos Aires, the town of Nova Colônia do Sacramento. Today Colonia remains Uruguay's gateway to Argentina, only thirty miles of water away. A treaty of 1750 gave Portuguese Colonia to Spain in return for Jesuit missions in Paraguay. A decade later, however, Portugal still had not turned over the Uruguayan port, causing Charles III of Spain to cancel the treaty. In 1762, when Spanish troops seized Colonia, they found twenty-seven English merchant ships anchored there, for Portugal had not been as determined as Spain to keep the British from sharing New World trade. Spain now controlled all of Uruguay, but a 1763 treaty again returned the Banda Oriental to Portugal.

Masterminding the diplomatic musical chairs whereby Uruguay again became a Brazilian region was Portugal's prime minister, the Marquis of Pombal, who utilized the support of Britain. In a continuing international military and trade soccer match, Colonia was a political soccer ball, passed back and forth between the Portuguese and the Spanish. Before the end of 1777, a new treaty suspended the fighting and permanently gave Colonia to Spain.

Inasmuch as 1776 found the British confronted by rebellious North American colonies calling themselves the United States,

England could no longer give unlimited support to Portugal against Spain. In that same year, Spain finally separated the vast lands of the Plata region from the distant control of the Viceroy of Peru in Lima, creating the Viceroyalty of La Plata to cope with the military and economic challenges of Portugal.

Larger Buenos Aires naturally became La Plata's viceregal seat, relegating Montevideo and the entire Banda Oriental to a subordinate status, which, a half-century later, would serve as the psychological impetus for Uruguay to assert its independence from both Argentina and Brazil.

THE BRITISH ARE COMING!

As in North America, so too in Uruguay, the colonists could cry "The British are coming!" But North Americans in 1775–76 were sounding an alarm against those who would reimpose a European monarchic yoke on the New World freedom fighters, whereas Uruguayans in 1805–7 had not yet loosened the Spanish chains that bound them to the motherland. English ships with only 1,600 British soldiers and marines sailed into the estuary to take Buenos Aires from a 9,000-man Spanish army. The cowardly, bumbling Viceroy of La Plata fled from Buenos Aires to Córdoba, in northern Argentina, before the first British platoon had landed. Other leaders, native-born Argentines, regrouped the Spanish forces and recaptured Buenos Aires.

Early in 1807, the British took Montevideo and held it for seven months. During a half-year occupation the British implanted two ideas among Uruguayans: the concept of a buffer state exploiting the rivalry of two large neighbors for its own internal security and the ideal of a free press.

On May 23, 1807, Brigadier General Sir Samuel Auchmuty personally opened the offices housing Latin America's first uncensored printing press, *The Southern Star—La Estrella del Sur*, with alternate columns of English and Spanish. The *Star* published for only eight weeks, but Latin America's first free press sowed the seeds of independence and gave Uruguayans a firsthand introduction to a few political liberties unknown before under Spanish colonial rule.

A REPUBLIC IS BORN

In 1808 Spain wore the yoke of France, with puppet king Joseph Bonaparte enthroned by the invading French troops of his brother Napoleon. In Montevideo, Javier Elío, commander of Spain's military forces, enforced a caretaker government independent of that of Buenos Aires. When full-scale fighting erupted in 1810 between South Americans and Spaniards, Montevideo refused to recognize the authority of the junta of Buenos Aires against the Spanish crown, Uruguay superficially continuing its allegiance to the mother country. However, the spirit of revolution grew in the hinterlands of Uruguay, and in 1811 rural Uruguayans launched a countermove against the Montevideo political posture of adherence to Spain.

José Gervasio Artigas, the leader of rural Uruguayans inflamed with the ideal of independence, became the father of Uruguayan nationhood. Not as well known outside Latin America as Simón Bolívar, Artigas nevertheless projected just as heroic an image. Artigas, a gaucho, had learned the art of warfare when he helped oust British occupation forces in 1807 as a commanding officer of a garrison of Spanish troops in the interior.

On May 25, 1810, a new ruling junta in Buenos Aires announced its sovereign right to govern the viceroyalty, and sent agents to the other cities of the far-flung La Plata colonial entity for participation in the new government. When Montevideo denounced the emissary from Buenos Aires, warfare between the two cities began, and would erupt again and again until Buenos Aires conquered Montevideo in 1814.

In 1811, Artigas led a gaucho cavalry against Spanish fortifications guarding Montevideo. Elío, commander of the Spaniards, called in Portuguese reinforcements from Brazil by sea and over land. Montevideo had been saved for Spain from Artigas' Uruguayans at the cost of having the remainder of Uruguay occupied by Portugal's Brazilian troops. Not until 1812 could the Portuguese be persuaded to withdraw northward, when Montevideo and Buenos Aires put into force a treaty of coexistence.

The new accord between Buenos Aires and Montevideo

prompted Artigas to withdraw far to the north, to Ayuí on the western bank of the Uruguay River in Argentina, opposite the town of Salto, Uruguay. A civilian wagon caravan of 13,000 people and 3,000 gaucho troops followed Artigas. Inasmuch as Uruguay's entire 1812 population totaled 60,000, this exodus represented one-fourth of all Uruguayans. From the exile encampment in 1813, Artigas authored a basic guide for the destiny of Uruguayans, the "Instructions of the Year XIII," found today in every primary school of the republic. These "Instructions" demanded a firm declaration of the independence of the united provinces of La Plata from Spain, to be followed by a confederation as the only acceptable form of governmental organization.

When the Buenos Aires assembly denied seats to the delegates from the Banda Oriental, Artigas decided to lead his troops southward again into triangular warfare among Uruguayans, Spaniards, and Argentines. In June, 1814, the commander of Spain's forces in Montevideo surrendered the city to an Argentine general, thereby permanently ending Spain's dominion in Uruguay. Now the struggle narrowed to a fight between the forces of Artigas and those Uruguayans and Argentines loyal to the regime in Buenos Aires. Early in 1815 Artigas forced the Buenos Aires troops out of Uruguay.

In 1817, once again a Portuguese army from Brazil captured Montevideo. After four years of fighting Brazilian invaders who outnumbered his Uruguayans three to one, Artigas suffered a final, bloody defeat. In September, 1820, Artigas took refuge in Paraguay, where for the next thirty years he would scratch out a living on a small farm. There, on September 23, 1850, Artigas died. The once inspired general and spirited gaucho had grown old as a farmer in obscurity, 1,000 miles from his homeland. Artigas' exile ended most resistance to the Portuguese, and a weak Uruguayan congress in 1821 formally annexed the Banda Oriental to Brazil as the Cisplatine Province.

In April, 1825, thirty-three Uruguayan patriots, led by Juan Antonio Lavalleja, crossed the river from Buenos Aires at night, to rally their countrymen against the Brazilian overlords. The small group, in this heroic gesture to free their country from a large Brazilian army, became the Immortal Thirty-Three of Uruguayan history. Each of the thirty-three leaders drew around him a group of fighting gauchos. For three years, a few thousand Uruguayans harassed regiments of Brazilians. Finally, in 1828, with encouragement from Britain, both Brazil and Argentina recognized Uruguay as an independent nation, a buffer state between two large and jealous neighbors.

The gently rolling, well-watered plains that had sheltered large numbers of wild cattle only a few years after the Spaniards had first turned them loose gave rise to the Uruguayan gaucho riding the range in pursuit of some of the world's finest livestock and leading a vigorous life whose hallmark became freedom. A gaucho spirit played godfather to the political philosophy of independence of the 1820's, and continued to resound in the Uruguayan way of life through most of the century. The talented novelist W. H. Hudson, whose semi-autobiographical cowboy hero of *The Purple Land,* written in 1885, represented the soul of Uruguay, captured the love of freedom that would carry into the 1900's and serve as the embryo of Latin America's most democratic nation.

The new republic of Uruguay kept the word "eastern" in its official name, República Oriental del Uruguay, as part of its heritage as the Banda Oriental of the Uruguay River. Uruguay as a new independent nation in 1828 had fewer than 100,000 people, a majority of them gauchos on the cattle ranges or shepherds scattered over the grasslands. In the capital, Montevideo, a tiny educated elite groped uncertainly at forging a modern nation-state.

Long Live the Constitution!

On July 18, 1830, Uruguay promulgated its constitution, as crowds outside the constituent assembly shouted "Long live the Constitution!"—and the voice of the people proved prophetic. For that charter remained in force down to 1919, rare in an area of the world where most other nations have written a succession of constitutions in vain attempts to achieve representative government and social justice by proclaiming these ideals to be the law of the land. The constitution of 1830 provided the legal foundation for a modern nation-state. Uruguayan political factions were able to redivide the spoils of public office from time to time and to update basic public institutions without resorting to the writing of new constitutions.

Despite the dominance of the president in the various nineteenth-century administrations, the nation's leaders did adhere to the constitutional principle of congressional immunity from prosecution for debates within the halls of the legislature. Speech flourished as genuinely free expression within Uruguay's parliament long before it became a national norm for the mass media. This inviolability of legislators for even the most unpopular opinions expressed within the legislative assembly, even in the turbulent nineteenth century, helped the constitution of 1830 live long as the national legal foundation.

THE NEW TROY

As early as 1836, the nation found itself faced with two opposing forces—each having private gaucho armies that engaged the other in battle—that had grown out of Lavalleja's group, the Immortal Thirty-three. Manuel Oribe, one of the Thirty-three, had solidified around himself a group known as the Conservatives, or Blancos (Whites), from the color of ribbons that they wore. Opposing these were the Liberals, known as Colorados (Reds), from their identifying ribbon, led by Fructuoso Rivera. In February, 1843, Rivera, then president of Uruguay, reacted when the Argentine dictator Manuel Rosas supported the rival Blanco Party. Rivera branded Rosas a tyrant and declared war on him. Thus began what Uruguayan historians call "The Great War," an eight-and-one-half-year siege of Montevideo by the Blanco and Argentine forces. Blockades from the sea came and went, but the overland attacks continued without interruption, taking on the overtones of classic struggles of ancient history (in Paris, Alexandre Dumas was inspired to write a book called *Montevideo: A New Troy*).

Argentines from three dissident anti-Rosas provinces rushed to the side of the Liberals in Uruguay. And Italy's Giuseppe Garibaldi, who was very shortly to become internationally famous, came to Montevideo to fight for the Colorados under Rivera. Today Garibaldi receives the laurels of a national hero in Uruguayan textbooks.

The siege of New Troy grew beyond a struggle between Blancos and Colorados, Argentine-Uruguayan Conservatives versus Uruguayan Liberals. A political and military struggle had grown into a cultural and economic fight between capital city and countryside, between Montevideo and *campo,* between big-city residents and rural folks.

In 1851, the revolt of Argentine General Justo José Urquiza against dictator Rosas forced the withdrawal of Argentine pressure against Uruguay, and the siege of Montevideo at last was lifted. For the first time since 1843 the capital of Uruguay had full land connections to its interior, with no hostile forces in between. On October 8, 1851, a treaty was signed that formally ended the siege. Today Uruguay commemorates this peace by calling one of Montevideo's main thoroughfares Avenida 8 de Octubre, an extension of Avenida 18 de Julio, the main street reminder of the republic's first constitution.

The treaty did not end all foreign intervention. During the next sixteen years, General Venancio Flores, a Colorado, twice asked Brazilians to help him hold onto power. In return, Flores committed the Banda Oriental to join Brazil and Argentina against Paraguay in the War of 1865–70.

MEASURED PROGRESS

After the Paraguayan war, the unhappy Blancos again waged a civil war against the Colorados, but, in 1872, when it became evident that the Liberal forces could control the government indefinitely, both political parties and their military supporters came to terms. An era of measured progress began, as revolutions softened into mild *coups d'état* and became rare. Rustic *caudillos* were succeeded by regular army officers with formal education and city manners in the offices of president, cabinet minister, and departmental and municipal officials. A wave of European immigration, especially of Italians, brought a new variety and vitality to Uruguayan society. New schools increased the literacy rate.

During the last third of the nineteenth century, elections came at regular intervals, as prescribed by law, but with the incumbent party in each territorial department always winning. The Colorados continued to monopolize the national government and, under the 1872 agreement, the Blancos controlled the key offices and the police in four territorial departments. A brief civil war in 1897 expanded the Blanco provincial control to six departments.

Beginning in 1890, civilian presidents came into office, but the dimension of violence had not yet passed from the political scene. In 1897, Juan Idiarte Borda, an authoritarian civilian president, in attempting to become a dictator, made the army the basis of his political strength, and was assassinated. In accordance with the constitution, Juan L. Cuestas, president of the Senate, immediately became chief executive. Blancos and Colorados put down their arms and signed a pact promising all citizens their political rights. For the first time in Uruguayan history, a civil war had ended without vengeance. To promote peace, Cuestas gave rebel leaders $200,000 to distribute to ease the transition of Blancos back to civilian life.

Under the constitution of 1830, the legislature elected the president of the republic and, after the Colorados and Blancos agreed on the division of legislative seats and executive appointments, it elected Cuestas, in 1899, to a full term, which split the Colorados just enough and united the Blancos just enough to encourage two-party interaction. In 1903, the senators and deputies chose as president a Colorado who had been president of the Senate, José Batlle y Ordóñez.

ERA OF BATLLE

The day before his election, Batlle (pronounced *bahj-jay*) stated his program: peaceful coexistence for the two major political parties, social reforms for the average citizen, and modern public-administration methods for the government. The fourth civilian in a row to occupy the presidency since 1890, Batlle was born in Montevideo on May 21, 1856, into a prominent Colorado family. When José was twelve, his father became president of Uruguay, serving from 1868 to 1872. José Batlle had founded the newspaper *El Día* as the editorial voice of the Colorado Party and, a year later, in 1887, he became political chief of the department of Minas, the first of a long series of public posts, culminating in the presidency.

Batlle's election prompted Aparicio Saravia, Blanco leader, to launch a rebellion, which flared on and off for a year and a half. Convinced that the Blancos could not win the election scheduled for 1904, Saravia got Brazilian arms and formed an army in the department of Rivera. On Christmas Day, 1903, Saravia briefed all Blanco field commanders. The stage was set for the last great military struggle between the two political parties.

On September 1, 1904, at the Battle of Masoller, the Blanco rebels suffered a decisive defeat. The shooting stopped and for the next two-thirds of a century, until the present time, Blancos and Colorados have fought only verbally, deciding who shall gain public office at the ballot boxes and determining public policies within the halls of the legislature. This civil war had not been class warfare. Within the labor unions in Montevideo, Marxists and Anarchists called for a negotiated peace. Colorados and Blancos were fighting to ensure, each in their own way, that the other party would honor all facets of coexistence.

For the remainder of his first term, Batlle used his presidential powers to promote peaceful rivalry in the political arena. He got most Uruguayans to debate the merits of social reforms and economic modernity. Public issues no longer centered in the personalism of generals but in the positive and negative factors of working conditions—a shift from an emphasis on eight-month battles to talk of an eight-hour workday. Uruguay was coming of age politically.

Of the twenty-five governments that guided Uruguay from 1830 to 1903, nine were overthrown, two ended by assassination, one was terminated by serious injury, and ten successfully resisted one or more revolutions; only three of the twenty-five governments were free of attempts to prevent peaceful completion of the legal term of office. By contrast, from 1903 to the present time, only the coup of 1933 interrupted constitutional norms, and even that action left in power the legally elected president.

During the periods of Spanish colonial rule and early independence, Latin American leadership was centered in aristocrats who were conditioned by leisure and cynicism to cling to conservative political programs. Army officers, the higher Church clergy, and the larger landowners formed a socio-economic tripod upon which political power rested. This structure, in all the Latin American republics of the nineteenth century, including Uruguay, constituted a defense of established interests, holding back forces for change.

After a limited amount of progress toward civilian rule and an expanding economy, Uruguay entered the twentieth century ready for some great leader to challenge the forces of traditionalism. José Batlle proved to be that man. With an editorial pen and a politician's oratory, Batlle led his nation toward a total readjustment of the country's social and economic system, from the legacy of colonialism to modern democracy.

As with great men in other countries, Batlle was the product of his times. When he entered the presidency in 1903, Uruguay was still floundering in medievalism. By the time of Batlle's death in 1929, the republic had become Latin America's first welfare state and the most open society in the hemisphere south of the United States.

Social and Economic Reform Begins

In 1905, a Colorado legislator introduced a bill to liberalize the 1885 marriage-annulment law—which had been the first such law in Latin America—into a full divorce law. The updating would permit a woman to institute litigation for divorce on grounds of cruelty, though her husband could only sue chiefly on grounds of adultery. Through editorials and news stories in *El Día*, President Batlle championed the measure as a vehicle for giving women a status of dignity in place of their long-time legal exploitation.

Encouraged by Catholic Church officials, the more conservative Blancos delayed passage of the law by endless debate on technical details. But in 1907 the Colorados forced a floor vote in both houses of the legislature, and the broader divorce law replaced the 1885 version, putting Uruguay in the vanguard of all of Latin America in terms of the legal and economic emancipation of woman.

In 1905, by presidential decree, Batlle abolished the income tax on the salaries of all public officials below certain levels, the forerunner of an end to income tax in general. Not until 1961 would a full-scale income tax be re-established in Uruguay.

Batlle also symbolized government concern for the workingman, the infirm, the aged, and the young. Noting that outside Montevideo the other cities of the republic had only primary schools, Batlle authorized, in 1906, by presidential decree, the establishment of secondary schools in every city of the interior. Prosperity had produced rising private incomes and a government budget surplus, allowing Batlle to complete long-awaited public works.

In 1908, when the railroad employees' union lost its strike for better pay and shorter hours, Batlle's editorial column in *El Día* thundered: "Every strike is justified and it would be ideal if all strikes could be successful." The same theme—that the workers must get better working conditions and a fairer share of the money that they helped the companies earn—began to recur in most Batlle speeches, writings, and proposals.

Batlle did not embrace a militant socialism that would take from the rich and give to the poor via taxation or confiscatory means. He stated flatly that the government should not break up large ranches but, rather, let various modern economic forces encourage a more equitable utilization of landed estates.

The constitution stipulated that a chief executive could not serve two consecutive terms in office. So Batlle prepared to step down from his 1903–7 term and then offer himself as a candidate for the 1911–15 term. He specified that, if re-elected in 1911, the first plank in his platform would be an eight-hour workday. And as soon as Batlle did get back in office in 1911, he sent to the legislature a message calling for a law setting the maximum workday at eight hours. As if to emphasize the need, the transit-workers' union began a strike to reduce their workday of fourteen hours. Batlle had to fight for four years more, into 1915, to get the eight-hour workday established in Uruguay, at a time when the remainder of Latin America seemed content to accept the age-old dawn-to-dusk workday with little or no organized protest.

Economic Reform: Government Corporations

Batlle urged the legislature to create government corporations, so that public entities could compete with private corporations in supplying certain vital goods and services, thereby getting prices within the purchasing-power range of the average citizen. Also, government corporations could lessen Uruguayan dependence on foreign companies in certain basic areas of national economic life.

The President petitioned the legislature to create a public entity to underwrite insurance and to popularize the purchase of life and fire insurance by the working class at lower rates than the commercial companies were offering. Batlle felt that government insurance would also pave the way for a nationwide system of social security benefits for the aged and the incapacitated.

In 1911, there were thirty-five private insurance companies doing business in Uruguay, twenty-six of them foreign firms. On January 11, 1912, the law went into effect establishing the State Insurance Bank, the *Banco de Seguros*. By 1936, this government agency was writing three-fourths of the insurance being issued in the republic. Most Uruguayan sources describe the field of insurance as a state monopoly, but that classification is not accurate. The 1912 law exempted private foreign companies already established in Uruguay from being curtailed. British insurance companies in Uruguay since the 1890's are still very much active today.

In the 1960's, any new welfare benefits involved with insurance added to the operations of the Insurance Bank, but the construction business required the special services of another entity, the

State Mortgage Bank, which began operations in 1892 as a private enterprise and became a government bank in 1912. Thus, today, when the president and the legislature consider basic policy changes in credit for housing construction, two specialized government banks are among the key consulting parties.

Batlle also successfully lobbied for publicly owned electric power. A 1912 law created the State Electric Facilities monopoly for the generation and distribution of electricity throughout the republic. Private enterprise had introduced electric lighting into Uruguay. In 1886 Marcelino Díaz y García established the first electric-light plant in South America. Montevideo and Buenos Aires across the Plata estuary were the first two cities in Latin America with electric street lights at a time when other large cities south of the United States still relied on gas lamps. Not making a profit, the company did not expand its service. Industrial demands for electricity were not met, and by 1905 most hotels and large factories generated their own power. Batlle used these facts in arguing for a state monopoly.

In 1915, the government undertook to own and operate the nation's telephone services, changing the name of the electric-power corporation to *Usinas Eléctricas y los Teléfonos del Estado*, or State Telephone and Electrical Facilities, better known as UTE. Because of deficit spending, the rates for telephone service have been kept low, and by 1954 Uruguay's per capita telephone ratio was second only to that of Argentina in all of Latin America and in 1965 it surpassed its neighbor.

Under a 1916 law, another Batlle reform created the National Administration of the Port of Montevideo, a state entity to operate the vast port facilities vital to the nation's foreign trade. Railroads remained in private hands until 1949, and a national airline did not come into being until 1936, long after Batlle's passing. But in the realm of banking, which made vital loans to the nation's transportation industries, again Batlle's stance in favor of government activity evidenced itself.

As he surveyed the weak spots in the economy, one of Batlle's concerns was rural credit. On the recommendation of the President, a 1912 law created a Department of Rural Credit within the Bank of the Republic. A postal savings system, created by a 1919 law, guaranteed that deposits could not be attached arbitrarily, specifying that women could deposit and withdraw without the consent or knowledge of their husbands—another Batlle reform for equal rights for women.

Political Reform: Plural Presidency

After his first presidential term, Batlle spent four years in Europe. In Switzerland, he discovered that a plural presidency had replaced a one-man chief executive. This governmental form tended to obviate the possibility of an authoritarian leader ruling as a strongman, the *caudillo* whom Latin America historically relied upon during crises.

Back in office for his second term of 1911–15, Batlle at first settled for smaller reforms, such as a modern copyright law, an urbanization plan for Montevideo, and the outlawing of bull-fights as inhumane in 1912. In 1913, the President proposed that Uruguay adopt the Swiss system of a collegiate head for the executive branch of government. This *colegiado* would guard against dictatorship and promote democracy.

The startling proposal provoked violent reaction, splitting the Colorado Party into factions that would persist down to the 1966 elections, fifty-three years later. The opposition Blancos naturally opposed the reform too, for, if they were to continue to symbolize an alternative to the Colorados and not an echo, they could not openly agree with the most vibrant Colorado personality of all time. Thus began Batlle's biggest battle.

A constituent assembly was elected to draft a reform constitution. But some Colorados and most Blancos stalled on putting the *colegiado* into final form. When Batlle threatened to run for a third term beginning in 1919 if his collegiate plan were not adopted before then, the Blancos and the dissident Colorados gave in, rather than face the invincible vote-getter.

His fight for a new constitution with a collegiate executive had overshadowed all else during the closing years of Batlle's formal leadership in office, but its adoption in 1919 did not end his active public life. For another decade, Batlle spoke out on public issues. The former chief executive even returned to a government post, for in 1920 and again in 1926 he presided over the National Council of Administration, the plural presidency he had created. The factionalizing of the Colorado Party deepened in the 1920's and, toward the end of his life, Batlle's grip on the party lessened. But, if his leadership waned toward the end of his life, it bounced back more potently than ever after his passing. All factions of Colorados to this day propose platforms in the name of *Batllismo*.

On October 20, 1929, Batlle died, confident that his social reforms had become part of Uruguayan life. Social security, public education for all, and various welfare benefits had kept the Uruguayan citizen from feeling alienated in his own land, as many other Latin Americans were. Batlle had ushered in a separation of Church and state under the 1919 constitution and had attempted to secularize concepts that extended back into Spanish colonial years, when Cross and Crown were entwined to the detriment of both. And yet, the Sisters of Charity attended him during his last days in the hospital and led the prayers for him as his body lay in state in the ornate marble Legislative Palace.

Batlle cast a lengthened shadow across his nation, dwarfing most of his critics and political opponents. Thousands of ordinary citizens waited in long lines in front of the Legislative Palace to pay their respects as the former President rested in state. Forty years after his death, Uruguayans are still commemorating him as the symbol of social justice.

III

Democracy's Challenge

The new charter, a compromise between partisans of a chief executive and supporters of collegiate government, as fought for by Batlle, went into effect in 1919, thus beginning Uruguay's experiment with a unique government structure. The constitution brought into being a two-headed executive branch. It divided executive responsibility between a president and a National Council.

The president was to be directly elected for a four-year term by a simple popular plurality. He would have the power to appoint the ministers of foreign relations, war-navy, and the interior. The National Council of Administration, a popularly elected body of nine members, was to be renewed by thirds every two years, when three of its members would be elected. The Council would control the ministries of public instruction, industry, labor, finance, public works, public welfare, and public health. This vertical bifurcation loomed as a unique governmental device not only in Latin America but also in the world.

During the prosperous 1920's, presidents and councils could toss problems back and forth in an economic atmosphere of rising incomes and employment. But, when the economic depression of the 1930's hit Uruguay hard, the division of government power led to a major political crisis.

MILD COUP

In 1933, as unemployment soared, President Gabriel Terra, frustrated by the inaction of the National Council, removed it from power in the only *coup d'état* of this century in Uruguay. Troops prevented members of both the legislature and the National Council from meeting. For the first time in the memory of the adult citizenry the government temporarily censored newspapers. The April 2 and April 3 issues of *El Día* carried pictures of former President Brum, who had committed suicide to protest the coup, but no word of his death. Police deported the dean of the law school of the University of the Republic, Emilio Frugoni, leader of the Socialist Party, though most citizens who were arrested were soon released. A few civil servants who led rallies protesting Terra's actions found themselves suspended from work.

Terra's coup was relatively mild—no deaths resulted and most liberties were preserved—but he did act unilaterally, to combat unemployment and the depressed state of the national economy. Without the delaying tactics of the National Council of Administration, the President reduced salaries of government employees, cut nonessential spending programs, added new programs to create jobs in depressed areas, and otherwise waged his own war on poverty. When Luis Alberto de Herrera, leader of the National Party (the former Conservatives, or Blancos) pledged cooperation, a coalition of moderately conservative Colorados and Blancos drew together enough dissident factions to give the new regime a semblance of nationwide backing.

The president announced a new coalition cabinet plus several expediters to speed up administrative procedures. José Serrato, president of Uruguay in 1923–27 and a widely popular Colorado, accepted the chairmanship of the board of the Banco de la República, thereby giving Terra the cooperation of various financial experts. Pedro Manini y Ríos entered the cabinet, giving the President the backing of another large segment of Colorados. Written messages from more than 100,000 citizens assured the president that he had helped prevent a violent revolution during the worst economic crisis in the history of the nation.

Just before Terra had taken office, the government deficit had zoomed to 1.5 million pesos a month, with public and private corporations rushing into bankruptcy. Exports of wool and mutton had sunk to all-time lows and unemployment rose to an all-time high. After Terra began to expedite import-export innovations and to make judicious use of public funds, relative economic prosperity began to return. By 1938 employment had risen enough so that most citizens could forgive the police action that had loomed as un-Uruguayan in the light of the 1904–33 traditions of political liberty.

THE CONSTITUTION OF 1934

Terra did not wish to function indefinitely in the illegal atmosphere of a suspended constitution. A basic charter institutionalizing a regime without the National Council of Administration had to be brought into being. In 1934, a constituent assembly wrote a new constitution, restoring a traditional one-man presidency. But this charter, in order to achieve Blanco support for Colorado President Terra, created a thirty-member Senate permanently divided by specifying that fifteen senators had to be Colorados and fifteen Blancos. Thus, although in subsequent elections the Colorados continued to have a popular majority, the Blancos received fifteen senators by constitutional default.

The constitution of 1830 had lasted eighty-nine years; the constitution of 1919 had functioned for fourteen years; but the constitution of 1934 remained in force only eight years. In 1942, President Alfredo Baldomir had it replaced with a new charter. One factor in Baldomir's move was centered in foreign policy, as World War II was raging. Uruguay had declared its solidarity with the United States as one of the Allies. Yet half the Senate under the Blancos could keep the president from carrying out Uruguayan commitments to the war effort.

Late in January, 1942, Uruguay decided to break relations with the Axis powers. The scuttling of the German warship *Graf Spee* in Montevideo harbor in 1939 and a plot of Nazis to seize the government in 1940 had rallied Uruguayan popular support for President Baldomir's pro-Allied position. Even after Uruguay broke with the Axis, some Blancos in the Senate continued to obstruct the government's measures to aid the Allies. The result was that the constitution of 1942 changed the charter mainly by eliminating the evenly divided Senate.

BATLLISMO MAKES A COMEBACK

In 1946, the Colorado electoral list headed by Tomás Berreta for president and Luis Batlle Berres for vice-president won. Berreta, an old man in ill health, died a few months after his inauguration, and the nephew of José Batlle, Luis Batlle, became president. The public became aware of a genuine split in the Colorado ranks in 1948 when Luis Batlle announced that he was establishing his own daily newspaper, *Acción,* to support the faction of the party known as List 15. The more traditional wing of the Colorado Party, List 14, was supported editorially by the newspaper founded by José Batlle, *El Día,* now run by his sons, César and Lorenzo Batlle Pacheco.

The rival factions of Colorados became known as *Quincistas* (Fifteeners) and *Catorcistas* (Fourteeners). Luis Batlle's faction would continue to grow until it became the dominant group within the Colorado Party in the 1950's. Meanwhile, during the late 1940's, the Blancos were gaining new members from the rural areas, citizens alienated by the urban orientation of the Colorados. And in the cities, the National Party also increased with numbers of political moderates disenchanted with Colorado preoccupation with organized labor.

By the time the 1950 presidential election was held, the Blancos had organized so well that their long-time leader, Luis Herrera, felt he would at last become chief executive, but for the sixth time he was defeated, partly due to the Uruguayan election system. The system is called the *lema* electoral process. The word *lema* literally means "motto," and each recognized party is identified by a *lema.* Factions of parties, however, can put forward a separate list of candidates identified by sub-*lemas.* After the votes are counted, the factions can pool their votes for a single party total. In 1950, the Colorados had three factions and the Blancos had two. But the Independent Nationalists, a Blanco sub-*lema*, decided not to pool votes with the faction headed by Herrera, and a Colorado president, Andrés Martínez Trueba, was elected.

Followers of the philosophy of José Batlle rejoiced, for President Martínez Trueba in his inaugural address on March 1, 1951, spoke of the need to revive the *colegiado* and share the presidency with the opposition Blancos. In 1951, therefore, leading Colorado and Blanco editorial voices found themselves on the same side. *El Día* and *Acción* for the Colorados and *El Debate* and *El País* for the Blancos each campaigned for a return to the collegiate system. A formal pact between the *Batllistas* and the *Herreristas*, on July 31, 1951, ensured that the major Colorado and Blanco factions would favor the constitutional reform. The legislature endorsed it and called for a plebiscite.

Sunday, December 16, 1951, was a pleasant, sunny summer day. Yet, despite mild weather and months of debate inside the legislative assembly and in the newspapers, less than one-half of the 1.1 million registered voters went to the polls. The *colegiado* just barely won approval. Out of a vote total of 429,760, the reform constitution carried by only 34,392 votes.

On March 1, 1952, the *Consejo Nacional de Gobierno*, or National Council of Government, took office. The 1952 constitution incorporated few new features not found in the charters of 1919, 1934, and 1942, except that every mention of the presidency had been replaced by *colegiado*. This National Council would serve out the presidential term of Martínez Trueba, who had been elected in 1950 for four years ending in March, 1955. The chairmanship of the nine-member Council was to be rotated annually among the six majority-party members.

At first, the National Council seemed able to solve the problems confronting the executive arm of government. In September, 1952, the city transportation workers of Montevideo engaged in work stoppages to back up their wage dispute with the municipality. When violence erupted, the National Council quickly agreed to ask the legislature for special powers to maintain law and order.

That authority was granted, the legislative branch acting as swiftly as the executive branch in facing the crisis. The strike was broken, the riots ended, and the buses again kept the residents of the national capital on schedule.

Again in 1958, a successor Council acted forcefully when law and order seemed threatened. Students at the University of the Republic, in supporting new organic laws, lapsed into acts of violence. Again the National Council, without delay, utilized the police to restore peace, so that the controversy could be resolved legally.

In both these challenges, the problem had been a straightforward situation: dissidents had openly resorted to violence, without any pretense of legality. Therefore, with lines of conflict clearly drawn, the Council could act without delay. But when complex social and economic crises arose, the National Council of Government hesitated, allowing its own internal factionalism to paralyze the highest executive authority.

ECONOMIC CRISIS

In the spirit of government by committee and coparticipation by both major political parties, the National Council in the 1950's appointed key officials of the public corporations in a ratio of three Colorados to two Blancos or four Colorados to three Blancos. It made for interparty harmony but it engendered an inefficiency in the operation of the nation's telephone and electric service, railroads, airline, postal service, and other government-owned and -operated entities.

At the very time that the world prices for wool and meat—Uruguay's principal exports—began to go down, the number of unnecessary employees added to public payrolls began to go up. Deficits plagued the national budget, dwindling the republic's gold reserves, as subsidies continued to rise to underwrite unprofitable public services.

Despite increased government spending, consumer inconvenience grew. For example, in June, 1958, all fruit and vegetable retailers and wholesalers in Montevideo boycotted the city's markets, trying to get the plural presidency to change policies of the Subsidies and Price Control Council. For a decade the Subsidies Council had underwritten the price of food produced by cooperatives, to force competing private retailers to keep prices down. When a president of Uruguay had been in office, the government frequently had ordered the Subsidies Council to change course when the economy experienced sharp upturns or downturns. But the faction-ridden National Council of Government seemingly could not agree even among its six-member majority to do so. After one week of no vegetables or fruit sold in Montevideo, the Subsidies Council itself adjusted cooperative prices so as not to force retailers out of business. But the collegiate government, to whom the general public and disputants had turned for advice, had not even issued a statement on the problem.

Similar crises involved milk, meat, and other basic consumer foods. Again and again in the late 1950's, the National Council of Government pondered instead of taking action, as the suffering general public grew increasingly restive. Historian Milton I. Vanger considered the National Council's economic policy regarding wool during the 1952–54 period to be realistic, but unsuccessful, because of a lowering of the world wool prices.* Again in 1957 the wool market shrunk and the economy suffered.

In prosperous times, the growing welfare programs could be financed from the wool and meat exports, with enough profit margin to permit some inefficiency in both industry and government. But by 1958 this leeway seemed to vanish. The peso became so soft that it had little purchasing power. A price spiral caused more inflation, and then the cause-effect chain of new strikes and more wage increases brought new price rises followed by more inflation.

The Communists grew bolder in the atmosphere of economic and political frustration. After having been relatively quiet for several years, in 1958 the Communist Party lent its leadership

---

*Milton I. Vanger, "Uruguay Introduces Government by Committee," *American Political Science Review* (June, 1954), p. 510.

to student movements ripe for violence. In May, 1958, U.S. Vice-President Richard Nixon visited Montevideo. A symbol of Yankee misunderstanding of South American problems, Nixon's presence prompted student mobs to revive street violence in Montevideo, which had long prided itself on Uruguayan courtesy to foreign dignitaries.

A POLITICAL UPSET

The economic crisis of the 1950's had not at first channeled public frustration against the National Council of Government as a slow-moving instrument, but rather against the majority party. For ninety-three years, from 1865 through 1958, the Colorado Party had controlled the presidency (or National Council) and had a majority in the legislature. Thus, the biggest political upset of this century was the 1958 victory of the Blancos.

The *Liga Federal de Acción Rural* (LFAR), or Federal League for Rural Action, led by Benito Nardone, was a major factor in the Blanco victory. In 1954, LFAR had supported Luis Batlle's Colorados, but by 1958 Nardone had become a *Herrerista*, and he took the *Ruralistas* into the National Party with him. Scenting the sweet smell of success, Nardone pushed the LFAR farther to the political right. On November 30, 1958, there were 1.4 million Uruguayans eligible to vote, and more than 1 million actually did. One-half million voted for Blanco factions and 379,000 supported Colorado factions. The remaining 210,000 votes went to minor parties.

Nardone presided over the six-member majority of the National Council of Government, which took office March 1, 1959. On April 8, 1959, the eighty-six-year-old Blanco leader Luis Alberto de Herrera died. Till his death, and ever since he had founded the newspaper *El Debate* in 1931, Herrera had symbolized the National Party more than any other Blanco. He had been defeated for president six times, and was part of the *colegiado* during 1925–31 and 1955–59. In four decades as a Blanco leader, Herrera had seldom advocated any new programs, except the negative ideas of fewer welfare benefits and more centralized government. In his time, he had admired Mussolini's dictatorship in Italy and Perón's in Argentina. Herrera's mantle was now seized by Nardone. Not until Nardone's own death in 1964 would the National Party be free of reactionary encroachments into its more traditional, responsible conservative ranks. Moderate Blancos abounded, but they could not challenge the leadership of Herrera and Nardone.

Nardone's charismatic voice had endeared him to tens of thousands of listeners to his Radio Rural broadcasts. Audience surveys indicated that every time *Chicotazo* ("Crack of the Whip") —as Nardone was billed on the air—got in front of a microphone, his program outdrew all competing broadcasts. Utilizing historical patriotic symbols, Nardone presented himself as the *Artiguista,* carrying out the sacred traditions of the national hero, Artigas. Gauchos led his rallies, and Nardone exploited the flavor of the cattle country in his speeches, a style dear to rural and provincial masses.

ECONOMIC ERUPTIONS

With a Blanco majority, the National Council of Government moved no quicker than it had with a Colorado majority. Inflation continued to erode purchasing power. In August, 1959, a strike left the nation without telephone service or electricity for several days. In September, a twenty-four–hour general strike by 100 trade unions also emphasized new wage demands. And nature added to the economic problems, as a record rainfall flooded crop and grazing lands.

A June, 1959, decree of the National Council of Government created the *Junta Nacional de Carnes* (National Meat Board) , which tried to balance the needs of the governmental and private meat-packing plants, the Cattlemen's Association, the Meat Workers Federation, and the Federal League of Rural Action against the need to control exports and imports within a framework of anti-inflation fiscal policies. A number of people were at least talking about their problems, but the solutions seemed remote. The National Council ended price ceilings on meat, and more

Uruguayan cattle went to slaughterhouses instead of being smuggled across the Brazilian and Argentine borders. The supplies went up, but so did the prices.

A mission of the International Monetary Fund (IMF) pointed out that Uruguay had extended social benefits to almost all of its citizens by spending more than it could earn annually. Implicit was the need for a moratorium on subsidy increases. As soon as the IMF report became public, nationalistic politicians began charging that the IMF had tried to infringe on the republic's sovereignty. Eight years later, in mid-1967, the same voices would be hurling the same charges against another IMF team of economists for again stating the truth, that the nation had overextended itself economically.

In response, the National Council requested that the legislature enact a monetary reform bill. As passed, this law simplified banking procedures and export-import trade, but production costs continued to rise. So did the cost of living. Minister of Finance Juan E. Azzini kept trying to get the National Council and the legislature to cut subsidies. But the retrenchment in public services resulting from such a policy was politically unwise. Communists in key positions in several unions were pushing a plan for a six-hour workday for the same salary then paid for an eight-hour workday, if management did not again raise salaries. Strikes came frequently.

ANOTHER BLANCO TERM

On November 25, 1962, an election chose the new National Executive Council and the legislature for four-year terms, and rejected a constitutional amendment to replace the Council with the office of president. More than 1.5 million voters had qualified to cast ballots, but only 73 per cent of them actually did. Beside the many party factions the debate also included the minor parties: Christian Democrats, Socialists, and Communists. The difference in vote totals between the two major parties shrunk to the lowest in history. The Blancos received a vote total of 472,317 and the Colorados 461,453.

In the 1962 campaign, the Blanco Democratic Union (UBD) and the orthodox *Herreristas* had forged a coalition. This group led by Víctor Haedo won more of the Blanco votes than did the Nardone-Ruralista faction. Therefore, when the new National Council took office on March 1, 1963, it had a Blanco majority of six, headed by Washington Beltrán of the UBD and Alberto Heber of the orthodox *Herreristas*. The Colorado minority was made up of Luis Batlle and Amílcar Vasconcellos of List 15 and Oscar Gestido of List 14. Four years later Vasconcellos would defend and Gestido would help end the collegiate executive system.

An Income Tax but No Solvency

In July, 1962, the government began collecting an income tax for the first time in decades and revenues began increasing, but Uruguay did not become solvent, for the National Council abolished a ban on imports. The import tax plus the new income tax could not counterbalance the national spending. The second Blanco administration of 1963–67 continued to suffer under inflationary pressures. Agricultural production stagnated at the levels of the 1950's. In industry, too much emphasis developed for products sold only inside Uruguay and not enough for products that could earn dollar credits abroad. Uruguayan economic life had become oriented toward consumption, without enough concern for production efficiency.

With the 1953 cost-of-living index serving as a base of 100, the index for 1965 had zoomed up to 2,395. Blancos traditionally symbolized conservatism, as contrasted with the Colorado image of political and economic liberalism. Yet, during the eight-year Blanco domination of government, budget deficits continued. Subsidies to unprofitable public enterprises were neither ended nor reduced.

From 1961 to 1967, the number of employees added to government corporations increased. One prime example was the government airline, *Primeras Líneas Uruguayas de Navegación* (PLUNA). Despite the campaign promises of the Blancos in 1958 and 1962, as fewer aircraft remained in service, the number of employees increased. By late 1966, PLUNA linked major provincial cities, but had cut back its operational aircraft from nine to six planes in daily use. Yet, during the same 1958–66 period, PLUNA had increased its personnel from 700 to 1,000, giving it more workers per operating airplane than any other airline in the world.

<h3 style="text-align:center">REVIVAL OF THE PRESIDENCY</h3>

In 1964, both Blancos and Colorados lost prominent leaders. Benito Nardone died, strengthening the leadership of Blanco factions other than his *Ruralistas.* Among the Colorados, the death of Luis Batlle Berres in July, 1964, did not diminish the vigor of his *Quincistas.* This List 15 became the Unity and Reform (*Unidad y Reforma,* or UyR) faction. The son of Luis Batlle, attorney and newspaper editor Jorge Batlle Ibáñez, took on his late father's duties as UyR leader. The death of César Batlle Pacheco, son of José Batlle, left his family in charge of *El Día* and General Oscar D. Gestido in control of the List 14 Colorados. This faction united with other moderates to form List 123, or the *Unión Colorada y Batllista* (UCB) faction.

Gestido, a graduate of the Uruguayan Military Academy, had headed the air force in the 1940's and, during 1949–51, took a leave of absence from military duty to be board chairman of PLUNA. He formally retired from military service in 1955, and served as chairman of the board of directors of the National Railroads during 1957–59. He became a member of the Colorado minority in the National Council of Government during 1963–66.

By 1966, Gestido had amassed almost twelve years of civilian experience as a public administrator, yet both the Blanco and rival Colorado factions accused him of being a militarist. And when, in the election of 1966, Gestido advocated a revival of the presidency, the daily *El Día* warned that, if voters returned a presidential system to solve economic problems, Uruguay would suffer "a *generalato* instead of the democratic *colegiado*"; that is, rule by generals would replace rule by the Council. Gestido anticipated the criticism of the Blancos, but the bitterness of rival Colorado attacks surprised him. Yet, after his victory, Gestido extended an invitation to many of these rivals to participate in the government.

The ballot for the November 27, 1966, election had a jumble of names and proposals. The voters would adopt or reject a new constitution whose principal change was the substitution of a president for the National Council of Government, and a municipal *Intendente* in place of each departmental council as provincial executive. The other major change was to increase the term of office from four to five years for all officials from president on down, including members of the legislature.

In a free-for-all, seventeen presidential candidates were on the ballot, some running both for the presidency and for the plural Council, in case the new constitution did not win approval. For example, Amílcar Vasconcellos, head of the Torch of Batlle faction of the Colorado Party, favored preserving the National Council. His slogan was: "Don't do it, but, if you do, do it for me"; that is, the voter was urged not to revive the presidency, but, if that did come about, then the voters should choose Vasconcellos as the new chief executive.

Despite the complex ballot proposals of five different versions of a new constitution and despite seventeen presidential candidates, some of whom embraced the National Council of Government but offered themselves for the presidency just in case, the vote counting followed Uruguayan electoral law; that is, what counted was the vote total of each party, not of each faction.

A total of 1,231,762 ballots were cast as follows:

Colorados	607,633
Blancos	496,910
FIdeL (Communists)	69,750
Christian Democrats	37,219
Socialists	11,559
Other minor parties	8,691

There were six Colorado factions, with Gestido winning 262,021 of the Colorado total of 607,633 votes, to become president under a new constitution approved by the voters.

THE GESTIDO ADMINISTRATION

When Oscar Gestido became president of Uruguay on March 1, 1967, he faced not only economic pressures, but the practical political problem of unifying the factions of his own majority Colorado Party. Gestido chose two UyR Colorados for his cabinet to cement relations between Jorge Batlle's faction and his own UCB. These appointees were Julio Lacarte Muró as minister of industry and commerce and Luis Hierro Gambardella as minister of culture (public education). Just four months later, both resigned as a result of the UyR faction's disagreement with economic policies.

Succeeding Lacarte as commerce minister was Zelmar Michelini, the 1966 presidential candidate of another Colorado faction. Only three and a half months later, Michelini also resigned, disagreeing with the president's use of emergency powers to curb Communist-led work stoppages that were crippling the economy. Carlos Manini Ríos, publisher of the daily newspapers *La Mañana* and *El Diario,* a former deputy and senator, and a past representative to the Organization of American States and the United Nations, succeeded Hierro. Manini Ríos brought the Gestido administration the kind of broad-based moderation and popularity that tended to strengthen it. Before the end of 1967 Manini became director of planning and the budget and in 1968 became president of the Bank of the Republic, as cabinet shifts continued.

As minister of finance, Gestido selected Carlos Vegh Garzón, an engineer with the National Fuel, Alcohol, and Cement Administration (ANCAP) before becoming board chairman of the Banco de la Plata and president of the Uruguayan Petroleum Institute. Vegh also left the cabinet in June, 1967, being replaced by Amílcar Vasconcellos. After only three and one-half months, in October, Vasconcellos resigned, protesting the presidential use of power to end work stoppages. Like his protesting ministers, Gestido also favored honoring constitutional liberties, but he disagreed with the libertarians on how to deal with Communist-led labor unions that abused the same open society that they hoped to bankrupt with strikes.

In October, Gestido ended a 117-day slowdown strike by bank employees and a four-month strike by the reporters, printers, and vendors unions against nine of the eleven Montevideo daily newspapers. The unions had been demanding a 36.5 per cent increase in pay to compensate for a 40 per cent rise in the cost of living during the first half of 1967. However, the unions were not asking for a July 1 base for the increment but, rather, a January 1 base, which in effect confronted management with a demand for a 76.5 per cent pay hike. After conciliation by the government, the unions settled for a 35 per cent pay increase, based on July 1 salaries.

One Gestido cabinet appointment proved to be especially helpful to his administration, that of Augusto Legnani as minister of the interior. In the centralized republic of Uruguay, all police came under the jurisdiction of the interior minister, who proved to have a subtle combination of tact and firmness in dealing with demonstrators. The former secondary-school history teacher and deputy utilized the police in keeping order in a manner that the general public overwhelmingly approved of, according to public opinion surveys. In May, 1968, Legnani resigned from the cabinet for health, not political, reasons. He had to undergo surgery and a long rest to recover his health.

One of Gestido's closest advisers was Héctor Luisi, an attorney whom the president appointed as minister of foreign relations. Chief planner for the Punta del Este conference of presidents of the Western Hemisphere in April, 1967, Luisi has been able to keep Uruguayan financial circles attuned to the exigencies of the world trade and Common Market concepts. In April, 1968, when the Senate summoned Luisi for an abrasive query into administration policies, he resigned. In January, 1969, he became ambassador to the United States.

Gestido took several bold steps to combat inflation. He got the legislature to pass a law allowing all citizens owing taxes to pay up promptly and thereby be forgiven penalties normally asked delinquent taxpayers. The response in payments became strong enough to surprise jaundiced critics who had long ago concluded that Uruguay could not escape its apathy and pessimism.

Gestido ordered his ministers of finance, interior, and commerce to cooperate in a government crackdown on contraband. Tax inspectors from the Finance Ministry, police from the Interior Ministry, and economists from the Commerce Ministry by mid-1967 began to display genuine teamwork. For the first time in years, Uruguayan motorists at the Brazilian border had to produce a valid title to automobiles suspected of not having had import taxes paid. And, for the first time in a decade, smugglers from Argentina began to have their boats and airplanes rounded up by Uruguayan police.

Contraband has not been eliminated but, after growing steadily from the 1950's, in 1967 and 1968 it at least began to lessen under more vigilant government action. But smuggling represents only one facet of lost taxes. Within the ranks of self-employed professionals, cheating on income tax returns and corporation taxes continues without severe punishment.

On November 6, 1967, the government devalued the Uruguayan peso 100 per cent, from approximately 100 pesos to the dollar to 200 pesos. This austerity action caused some domestic political outcries, but in world-wide economic circles the move, coupled with the effort by the Gestido regime to hold the line on spending, restored a measure of international confidence in Uruguay in the realm of foreign trade. Gestido vowed that further foreign debt would not be incurred and that the government would strive to stimulate production and would expect labor unions as well as civil servants to support programs to stabilize the currency.

Gestido used television effectively in rallying public opinion. His video image seemed to inspire rival Colorados and Blancos alike into new determination to pull the nation out of its economic crisis. Then on December 6, 1967, Oscar Gestido died of a heart attack, at sixty-six years of age. For nine months, since taking office on March 1, Gestido had worked strenuously to end the series of strikes and to halt inflation. He confronted Communist-led labor unions with firmness, within a framework of constitutional law, winning the esteem of Uruguay's democratic populace, whose traditions call for an open society of nonviolent protests.

Working seven days a week, Gestido was on the verge of persuading the unions and the legislature to support spending cuts by the government of up to 40 per cent to restore the purchasing power of the peso, when he died, literally in the service of his country.

THE PACHECO ADMINISTRATION

Vice-President Jorge Pacheco succeeded Gestido, to finish out his five-year term to March, 1972. A reporter and editor at *El Día* during the 1940's and the 1950's, Pacheco became executive editor during 1961–65, resigning to campaign for a revival of the office of president. Even though *El Día* itself clung to José Batlle's idea of an executive council or *colegiado,* many *Batllista* readers of the daily remained friendly to Pacheco. Senator Alberto Abdala became vice-president.

Like Gestido during 1967, Pacheco in 1968 suffered cabinet crises as strikes continued to erupt, eroding governmental opposition to pay raises, which have kept the inflation spiral going upward. Uruguay experienced 700 strikes during 1966 and the same number during 1967. The cost of living went up 88 per cent in 1965, 51 per cent in 1966, and 136 per cent in 1967. In 1950, the Uruguayan peso loomed as the most solid South American currency, steady at fifty U.S. cents. After the 1967 devaluation, it had slipped to one-half of one U.S. penny. And, like Gestido, Pacheco also had to call for a devaluation. On April 29, 1968, the rate dipped from 200 pesos to the dollar to 250. To offset price hikes on vital food products, the Pacheco administration then froze prices on more than 200 items, ranging from sugar to pork.

For a decade the economic problems have worsened. World prices for wool and meat—mainstays of the Uruguayan economy—have gone down as public and private debts have gone up. As with the National Council of Government and with the Gestido administration, the Pacheco government has found its most pressing problem to be the nation's swollen bureaucracy weighing heavily on the budget. Out of a total work force of 810,000, some 260,000 Uruguayans work either for the national or local government or for government-owned and -operated utilities and businesses. Some 250,000 Uruguayans are under social security pensions, some of them forty-five to fifty-five years old, adding to the strain on the public treasury and to the political stress when large numbers of citizens find their purchasing power on fixed incomes dwindling because of inflation.

Uruguayans do not want to undo the social legislation that has given them a dignity as individuals that their counterparts in many other Latin American nations have never known. With extensive public-health facilities, Uruguay leads Latin America in longevity, its 1968 estimate being sixty-three years of age. Thus, the older segment of the population grows within a high standard of living, adding more and more to the pension rolls.

President Pacheco has not been able to reduce either government payrolls or a budgetary deficit, which in 1968 was estimated at $3.9 million. Uruguay has $180 million in gold and foreign-currency reserves, but $500 million in long- and medium-term debts. And industrial peace, whereby increased production could revitalize the private sector of the economy, has remained only a fond hope. Communists, who occupy 80 per cent of the top offices in the fourteen most important unions, though they comprise only 3 per cent of the membership, have made the meat-packing plants, the docks, public-utility installations, and government offices their battleground in undermining the economy by means of strikes that demand wage increases that neither industry nor government can meet without increasing inflation. The slow-moving National Council of Government failed to cope with this problem. But a revival of the presidency under Gestido and Pacheco has not been able to restore industrial peace either.

President Pacheco has, therefore, tried to purge Communists from unions. In a nation steeped in civil liberties, he has had to exercise skill in confronting pickets and demonstrators. In May, 1968, Pacheco chose Eduardo Jiménez de Aréchaga as interior minister, one of Uruguay's most prominent jurists. The former law professor deployed police in a manner designed not to escalate public disturbances. But the strikes continued.

In June, 1968, students and labor union members battled

police, smashing windows and injuring civilian bystanders. Radical leaders encouraged a walkout by primary and high school teachers and some university professors, to protest increased living costs. Whereupon President Pacheco declared a state of emergency, allowing arrests of mob leaders, without a court order or warrant. In protest against this abridgment of constitutional civil liberties, three cabinet officers resigned—Public Health Minister Carlos Queraltó, Labor Minister Manuel Flores Mora, and Culture (Education) Minister Alba Roballo, the only woman in the cabinet—further splitting the Colorado Party's factions on the question of how forceful the chief executive should be in meeting the economic crisis.

In June, 1968, the President established price and wage ceilings, but by 1969 he agreed to some increases. The strikes continue, bringing new price and wage increases, which, in turn, continue the inflationary spiral.

In March, 1969, President Pacheco lifted security measures that had been in force for nine months. Police withdrew from corporations, which had been targets of Marxist-led unions and demonstrators. The small group of Communist terrorists, the *Tupámaros*, continue as a potential danger, however, for they claim as members 1,000 Montevideans who outwardly live as law-abiding citizens but secretly are ready for violence.

Pacheco has managed to turn debate among Colorado and Blanco factions from law and order procedures to economic recovery plans. Despite the stresses, Uruguay remains a democratic republic.

IV

Government and Political Organization

Since 1966, Uruguay has been a presidential republic. The president must be native born and at least thirty-five years old. Elected for five years, he cannot succeed himself in office. In case of death, resignation, or permanent incapacity, the vice-president serves out his term. If the vice-president spends more than one year as president, he then cannot run for the next term.

The president is charged with preserving law and order, is commander-in-chief of the armed forces, can deploy troops or the police anywhere inside the republic, or can dispatch troops abroad within the limits set by treaties or after the legislature has issued a declaration of war. He must deliver a "State of the Nation" message to the legislature every year and has the power to introduce bills directly. If the president proposes emergency bills to meet a specific crisis, each chamber of the legislature has forty-five days to consider passing, changing, or rejecting the measures. Should the ninety days expire without any congressional action, the president can automatically invoke his emergency power to deal with that specific crisis.

The president can call the legislature into special session and can veto a bill, although both houses of the legislature can override the veto by a vote of three-fifths of the members present, within sixty days after the veto. The president appoints all high-ranking military officers, diplomats, and judges with the confirmation of the Senate and is charged with enforcing all laws, with the police under presidential authority. Within six months of taking office, the president must present the legislature with the general budget for his entire five-year term. Changes are made in each annual working budget, however.

THE COUNCIL OF MINISTERS

The president appoints a cabinet of eleven ministers, collectively called the Council of Ministers. Each minister nominated must be approved by a simple majority vote in each chamber of the legislature. The president can ask any of his ministers to resign if they do not support his policies, and the Chamber of Representatives can suspend a minister from office by a two-thirds vote.

AUTONOMOUS ENTITIES

Some governmental functions, such as the airlines, the telephone service, and the fishing industry, are run by public corporations rather than cabinet ministries. These corporations either elect their own board of directors or the president of the republic nominates them, subject to confirmation by a three-fifths vote of the Senate. The legislature can, by a two-thirds vote in each chamber, change the top management of a public corporation from a board of directors to a director-general. Legislative approval is also required for private capital to participate in a public corporation, but private funds cannot exceed 50 per cent of the total capitalization of an autonomous entity. The legislature can create a new public corporation by a two-thirds vote of each chamber.

The 1966 constitution created a Central Bank, which cares for currency circulation, while a second government bank, the Bank of the Republic, concentrates on public and private credit. It also established an Accounts Tribunal, whose seven members are selected by the legislature for five-year terms. The Accounts Tribunal is responsible for checking on expenditures and the collection of revenues, investigating prices charged by public corporations, and reporting fiscal irregularities on all levels of government to the legislature.

The 1966 constitution also created the office of Director of the Budget and Economic Planning, with the status of a cabinet ministry, and the Council of National Economy, a purely consultative body (its members serving without salary) that recommends economic policies for the nation. An Administrative Tribunal hears allegations concerning administrative abuses, though questions of civil liability remain with the regular courts.

THE LEGISLATURE

The bicameral legislature is called the General Assembly. The basic function of enacting legislation is the principal role of the Senate, the upper house, and the Chamber of Representatives, the lower one. But, unlike many other Latin American nations where the president dominates the legislature, Uruguay has nurtured the tradition of legislative vigor during most of this century. In a nation steeped in traditions of free speech and representative government, each chamber has a large visitors gallery, often filled with citizens during debates on crucial issues. With rare exceptions committee hearings are open to the press.

Legislative sessions run nine months per year, from mid-March to mid-December. The Senate consists of thirty members, with the vice-president, who can vote as if he were a senator, presiding. The entire Republic of Uruguay constitutes the electoral district for senators. Based on the popular-vote totals, senators are chosen by a system of proportional representation. The total number of votes cast are divided by thirty-one, the number of senatorial votes. Thus, in 1966, 1,231,762 votes were divided by thirty-one for a quotient of 39,734. The number of senators elected from each party was determined then by dividing the total party vote by the quotient. The Colorados, with 607,633 votes, therefore, were entitled to fifteen senators.

There are ninety-nine representatives, or deputies, in the Chamber of Representatives. The National Electoral Court determines the number allotted to each territorial department before an election, using for its calculations the votes cast in the previous election plus the new registrants. After an election, the seats for representatives within each department are apportioned among the political parties by the same method used in distributing seats for the Senate. In the Chamber elected in 1966 there were 50 Colorados, 41 Blancos, 5 Communists, and 3 Christian Democrats; in the Senate, there were 17 Colorados, 13 Blancos, and 1 Communist. With proportional representation and with vote-pooling by party factions, this electoral system makes Uruguayan politics more moderate and personalistic than ideological and class-oriented.

For every candidate for deputy and senator a substitute is also nominated. A Uruguayan congressional candidate has his name coupled to a substitute. Uruguay is thereby spared the necessity of holding special elections to fill vacancies caused by death, illness, or resignation, and, when opportunity for advancement arises, a member of the General Assembly is not reluctant to surrender his seat for another appointment, since his party's strength is not affected by his resignation.

With the executive branch during 1952–66 unable to take a decisive lead in public policy because of the plural presidency, the legislature intensified its position as the primary arena of political decision-making. Each chamber conducts its major business in standing committees, but, in a practical sense, development of parliamentary legislation follows a series of agreements among party factions, then among the sub-*lemas* of a party, and finally among the major and minor parties. Both in committee hearings and in floor debate, a degree of bargaining and compromising takes place.

Representatives, though chosen from within departments, do not have to be residents of those districts. This has meant, in practice, that most members of the legislature have made their homes in Montevideo. With each chamber being urban-oriented, the legislature has not reflected adequately the interests of the provincial citizens. In the age-old battle of countryside, or *campo,* versus the capital, the latter controls the General Assembly not only by virtue of the voting strength of Montevideo, with half the

national population, but also because the lawmakers themselves are big-city residents.

THE JUDICIAL BRANCH OF GOVERNMENT

Latin American nations in general derive their legal systems from Roman law, whereas the United States has inherited British, or common, law. Like the other Latin American republics, Uruguay's primary and predominant source of law is the statute book, the laws enacted by the legislature. By contrast, in Anglo-American law, rivaling legislation as a primary source of law is the jurisprudence called case law, the precedents laid down by the courts and formulated by judicial decisions in specific cases. In the United States, Canada, and Britain, much of the law of contracts, for example, must be sought first in the reports of decided cases. Throughout Latin America, an attorney concerned with contracts would begin with codes coming from the statutes.

At the apex of the judicial branch of government is the Supreme Court of Justice. From 1818 to 1829, Uruguay's highest tribunal was called the Appellate Chamber, then it became known as the Appellate Tribunal, the Superior Tribunal of Justice, and the High Court of Justice. Finally, the 1934 constitution brought the Uruguayan judicial nomenclature into line with that of the other republics of the Western Hemisphere, proclaiming the highest judicial power in the land to be the *Suprema Corte de Justicia.*

The Supreme Court consists of five justices. A member must be at least forty years of age and, like all judges of the lower courts, must retire upon reaching seventy years of age. Justices serve a term of ten years and may not be re-elected for a second term until an intervening period of five years has elapsed.

Justices are chosen by the legislature by a two-thirds vote of the total membership of both chambers. When a vacancy on the Supreme Court occurs, the legislature must fill it within ninety days. Should the General Assembly not be in session or be otherwise occupied, a special session must consider qualified candidates. Should the legislature not be able to reach a decision, the Appellate Tribunal judge with the most seniority would then automatically move up the judicial ladder to become a Supreme Court justice.

Below the highest court of the republic are the Appellate Tribunals, each composed of three judges. To be eligible, a candidate must be at least thirty-five years old and have eight years experience as a practicing attorney or six years experience as a public prosecutor or lower-court judge. Below the appellate court are the Courts of Record, the basic courts of first instance throughout the republic for criminal cases and for civil suits involving more than small sums of money.

The Supreme Court justices select the judges of the Appellate Tribunals and the Courts of Record. For Appellate Tribunal positions, the nominees must also be confirmed by the Senate. Judges of the Courts of Record have life tenure, but must retire at age seventy. If convicted of illegal or immoral conduct, lower-court judges may be removed by the Supreme Court. Thus, the Supreme Court administers the whole judicial system.

At the bottom of the judicial ladder are the justices of the peace, who handle civil suits involving modest sums of money. In the department of Montevideo, a justice of the peace must be an attorney, but in the other departments he may be a public notary, whose status is similar to that of a notary in France. A notary must pursue a course of study at a law school only moderately less rigorous than that for an attorney. Justices of the peace serve a term of four years, but can be removed from the bench at any time for misconduct.

Uruguay enacted a Code for Minors in 1934 and revised it in 1938. This code provides for a Juvenile Court in Montevideo, with jurisdiction over offenders under eighteen years of age. Among the administrative duties assigned to the Juvenile Court is the inspection of institutions devoted to child welfare. The court may pass on the suitability of childless couples for adopting orphans. If evidence warrants, the Juvenile Court may remove children from foster homes and place them in public institutions. And, in recent years, this court has assumed the function of authorizing the enlistment of minors in the armed forces. The Juvenile Court is not a court of last resort; therefore, appeals from its decisions may be carried to the Appellate Tribunals of the basic court system.

A special court of Uruguay is the Electoral Court, having nine judges, plus substitute judges to fill any vacancy, chosen by a two-thirds vote of the total membership of each chamber of the legislature. Electoral Court judges cannot be candidates for any public office at the time that they are considered for appointment nor during their tenure in office. This court has authority over the administration of national elections and over the departmental electoral boards, which supervise voting within the nineteen provincial subdivisions of the nation. It has the duty to safeguard honesty and impartial conduct by polling officials, custody of the archives of election results and of the lists of registered voters, and the power to hear claims connected with disputed elections and to render a decision in such cases as the court of last resort.

LOCAL GOVERNMENT

Uruguay is divided into nineteen departments, and local government is departmental government. Under the collegiate system, from 1952–66, the departmental executive resembled its national counterpart, with a Departmental Council. Under the 1966 constitution, the capital city of each department has an *Intendente Municipal*, who serves both as mayor of that city and as governor of the surrounding department. Thus the *Intendente* of Montevideo functions both as the mayor of the city proper and as the chief executive of the surrounding department.

Each department has a legislature, called the *Junta Departmental* or Departmental Board, consisting of thirty-one members. Under the 1952 constitution, the department of Montevideo had a board of sixty-five members, but under the 1966 constitution its board contains only thirty-one members. During July and August, 1966, when the constituent assembly debated ways of streamlining local government to utilize better techniques in both departmental legislatures and executive offices, the unwieldiness of the old Montevideo board was condemned by both major political parties.

To be eligible to serve as an *Intendente,* a candidate must be at least thirty years of age and either a native of the department in which he will serve or a resident there for three years before he assumes office. Elected with the *Intendente* are four substitutes, who, in turn, could assume office in case a vacancy occurs before the five-year term can be completed.

In 1967, a political controversy arose when the elected mayor of Montevideo, Glauco Segovia, attempted to designate someone other than the first substitute as acting *Intendente* while he took a leave of absence to attend the International Conference of Municipalities in Barcelona, Spain. Opposition Blanco members of the Departmental Board objected, and on October 14 the Colorado *Intendente* resigned. He was succeeded by Carlos B. Herrera, who had been chosen in the November, 1966, election as first alternate to the mayor.

Each capital city has a municipal staff, the *Intendencia,* though of course Montevideo, with almost half the nation's population within or near its city limits, contains the most extensive staff. Its public works and engineering divisions maintain a vast network of streets, sewers, parks, and sanitation facilities. Either the Departmental Board or the *Intendente* can propose local taxes, but in either case the board must vote final approval. All acts of local governments can be vetoed by the national legislature, by the Accounts Tribunal, or by the Supreme Court.

Intendentes receive salaries but board members serve without pay. The nineteen mayors of Uruguay, serving in their capacity as chief executives of their departments, come under the administrative jurisdiction of the minister of the interior. When the minister of the interior wishes to coordinate some nationwide program in the various cities and towns—say, for example, new procedures for municipal police in guiding traffic—he can utilize a relatively simple mechanism of intergovernmental relations: he calls a conference with the nineteen *Intendentes* of Uruguay.

Although some Uruguayans have expressed a willingness to decentralize governmental decision-making, in practice at the local level specific movements in that direction have been modest. For instance, in 1951 the first municipal referendum election ever held in Montevideo dealt with increases in bus fares, seventeen years after such municipal referendums were first authorized. The device of a petition by voters to engender action on municipal matters is also provided for under the constitution, yet the initiative is not taken in practice.

CITIZENSHIP AND SUFFRAGE

Anyone born in Uruguay can claim Uruguayan citizenship, as can anyone whose father or mother was a Uruguayan citizen, regardless of where the offspring was born, as long as the parent or parents inscribe the baby's name in the Civic Registry (*Registro Cívico*).

After three years of residence in Uruguay, foreigners of good moral conduct who can prove that they possess the skill to pursue a trade or profession or who otherwise possess property sufficient to ensure a livelihood, can petition for citizenship, if their relatives are Uruguayan. If they do not have a family connection in Uruguay, the period of residence is five years before procedures can begin toward acquiring citizenship. A person must be eighteen years of age to be considered an adult citizen, able to exercise his full rights and duties.

Suffrage is extended to all citizens without restriction as to sex, race, or creed. In addition, foreigners who have resided in Uruguay for fifteen years, maintain a family in the republic, and can prove that they are gainfully employed in some profession or trade or possess sufficient capital to maintain a livelihood, may register to vote.

All Uruguayans eighteen years of age or older are obligated by law to register with the Civic Registry, except for the insane, criminals, and those totally handicapped physically. Thus, most adult Uruguayans are registered voters but are not forced to cast ballots. Voting must be secret and is obligatory for all citizens, though the requirement has never been enforced.

THE TWO MAJOR PARTIES

In 1836, during the Conservative-Liberal war, at the Battle of Carpintería, the leaders of both parties conferred under a flag of truce and decided that, to avoid shooting their own men because the groups wore no uniforms, the Conservatives would tie white kerchiefs around their sleeves and the Liberals would wear red ones. Hence, today, the Conservative Party—officially the National Party—still answers to the name Blancos (Whites) and the Liberals are on the ballot as Colorados (Reds). The colors in no way link the parties to political or ideological groups abroad.

During the two terms of President José Batlle, the Colorados split into two groups, those favoring and those opposing the Batlle idea of a plural presidency. As the more liberal of the two major parties, the Colorado factions together have drawn support more from urban than from rural groups, more from labor than from management, and have been the champions most of the social legislation of the twentieth century.

Under the long-time domination of Luis Alberto de Herrera from the 1930's until his death in 1959, the National Party tended to divide into anti- and pro-Herrera forces. With strength coming from the landowners, farmers, and ranchers, the Blancos have also drawn the support of business executives and the economic upper class in Montevideo. During the ninety-three years of Colorado governments, from 1865 through 1958, the Blancos developed the tradition of opposing many of the social reforms that the majority party initiated.

The fundamental unit of the factions of both major parties is the community club. Each club is an office and lounge, and party members who live or work in the neighborhood can meet there to coordinate political activities, to discuss job openings in government or private industry, or to chat over drinks.

THE MINOR PARTIES

Three minor parties, organized along tighter ideological lines than the multigroup Blancos and Colorados, are the Socialist, the Communist, and the Christian Democratic parties. Such ideological parties have a long history in Uruguay. The Socialist Party was founded in 1910, the Communist Party in 1921, and the Catholic Party in 1872. Yet minor parties have never been a major threat to the two principal parties. In recent decades, their combined vote has been less than 10 per cent of the total.

The Catholic Party, from its founding in 1872 to 1912, was mainly the organized opposition to the growing secular way of life that was modernizing Uruguay. The Catholic Church had long been in a relatively weak position compared to the rest of Spanish America. The absence of a ready source of wealth for construction of churches, found by Spanish colonial officials in mineral-rich Mexico and the Andean region, combined with the organizational subservience of the Church of Uruguay to the leadership of Buenos Aires, minimized colonial growth of clericalism in government.

In 1912, the old Catholic Party became the Civic Union, evidencing greater social concern and, recently, spurred by two papal encyclicals—*Mater et Magistra* and *Pacem in Terris* of Pope John XXIII—it has become even more dynamic. In 1962, it officially became the Christian Democratic Party, espousing a Christian socialization, emphasizing society as a community of individuals, and, without challenging private property rights, seeking a better economic distribution in the interests of the common good. In the 1966 election, the Christian Democratic Party elected three deputies to the Chamber of Representatives and captured approximately 3 per cent of the total vote.

The Socialist Party had already decayed when in 1962 it became part of a coalition, the Popular Union, electing two deputies. But the Popular Union soon unraveled, leaving the Socialist Party to campaign on its own in 1966, when it failed to elect even one deputy. By December, 1967, it had shrunk to a tiny group of a few thousand Maoists, calling through the party newspaper, *El Sol,* for guerrilla warfare. Under a 1940 law against parties seeking the violent overthrow of the government, President Pacheco, on December 12, 1968, dissolved the Socialist Party. Not only did a majority of Uruguayan groups—liberal and conservative—agree with his action, but even the pro-Moscow Communists rejected the violence sought by the Socialist Party in its dying days.

The Communist Party is the outgrowth of a split in the socialist ranks after the Russian Revolution. Socialist Party founder Emilio Frugoni strongly opposed pro-Soviet sentiment. In 1919, pro-Soviet elements were found mostly in the maritime unions, led by Eugenio Gómez. In 1921, in the first Uruguayan Communist daily newspaper, *Justicia*, Gómez urged affiliation with the Third International as a gesture of solidarity with the Russian Revolution. Many socialists then withdrew from the Gómez group to rejoin Frugoni in rebuilding a Socialist Party.

In the 1920's, the Communists founded a labor newspaper, *Red Trade Union*, and began to build a labor federation. By the 1960's, although Communists represented only a small minority of the ranks of organized labor, they were entrenched in the top offices of major unions, fomenting hundreds of strikes annually.

With the outbreak of World War II, in 1939, the Communist Party adopted the Moscow line, denouncing the Allies and organizing "peace" marches. In 1941, after having opposed the war against Hitler in the spirit of the German-Soviet nonaggression pact, the Uruguayan Communists had to do an about-face when the Nazis invaded the U.S.S.R. This switch caused a serious split in the party and widespread public criticism.

A second noticeable public jeer at the Uruguayan Communists came in 1967 when again they did an about-face. Uruguayan Communists had long proclaimed how they deplored anti-Semitism and how they favored Jewish as well as other minority aspirations in various parts of the world. Then, during the last week in May, 1967, as Nasser of Egypt threatened to drive every Israeli into the sea, the voice of the Uruguayan Communist Party, the daily newspaper *El Popular*, suddenly became not only anti-Israeli but also anti-Jewish. After Israel's quick military victory in June, *El Popular* began to editorialize against Israel, but many non-Communist leftists deluged other publications with pro-Israeli sentiment, and liberal Catholics began to display pro-Israeli signs. On June 12, 1967, the Central University Council voted a declaration that the state of Israel had a right to exist in peace and that all nations should work to end the state of belligerency in the Middle East.

Again the Uruguayan Communist Party had a silly and negative public image.

Communist influence among some students and working-class adults has been achieved through the Uruguayan-Soviet Institute and the Uruguayan-Cuban Culture Institute, centers ostensibly organized to promote cultural understanding. Most successful Communist penetration into Uruguayan public life has been through offices held by party members in the key labor unions.

In general elections, the Communist Party did not draw any attention until 1946. Even in the 1958 election it received only 2.7 per cent of the total vote. But, in 1962, by forming an alliance with other far-left groups, the Communist Party became the central and controlling factor in the *Frente Izquierda de Libertad* (FIdeL), or Leftist Liberty Front, capturing 3.5 per cent of the total vote and electing one senator and three deputies. In the 1966 election, with 6 per cent of the total vote, FIdeL elected one senator and five deputies, reaching its greatest political strength since the founding of the party in 1921.

The voting behavior of Uruguayans in this century has been that of political moderates who have rejected extremes. The Communists have not been able to engulf Uruguay at the polls, but their party has gained some supporters among the dwellers in the old slums of Montevideo and among the unemployed living in the urban shantytowns. In terms of shaping or influencing any public policies, however, the Communists rely on their strategic positions within labor unions.

MILITARY FORCES

Elsewhere in Latin America, the armed forces take on a political importance; but, in Uruguay, the role of the military remains nonpolitical. In time of disorder, the small but modern army backs up the national police as a reserve constabulary force, but operates well within the confines of constitutional law, guarding strike-bound docks or utilities upon presidential command, with a courtesy and self-restraint for civilian pickets that makes the term "police brutality" absent from the Uruguayan political vocabulary.

The army of 10,000 consists of a professional officer corps of graduates of the National Military Academy and the enlisted ranks of volunteers. An organized reserve of 120,000 uses regular-army facilities once a month, as well as during a summer-camp period. No selective service operates, yet every vacancy in the ranks fills easily, for, after fifteen years of active service, an enlisted man or an officer can retire on a pension based on his highest rank. Thus, a seventeen-year-old recruit can look forward to a pension at age thirty-two, when he is young enough to launch a civilian career underwritten by his military pension. Volunteers may also sign up for one- or two-year tours of duty.

The small navy has 350 officers and 1,500 enlisted sailors. In addition, the naval air service maintains three bases in continual readiness for sea rescues. The navy has been successful in training units of the police in Montevideo, Punta del Este, and other crowded port areas in sea rescue and harbor patrol work. Navy planes are still the U.S. piston-engine fighters and bombers built in the 1940's and 1950's.

The air force, however, has modernized, having a fighter-bomber squadron equipped with Lockheed F-80 Shooting Star jets, plus older bombers, fighter planes, and T-33 jet trainers.

The armed forces have somewhat of the civic image of firemen in the United States, not only being trained for rescue work and first aid, but also being active in repairing and distributing toys to needy children at Christmas and helping in campaigns directed by the Red Cross for blood donors.

During the time of the Perón dictatorship in Argentina, a handful of Uruguayan army officers seemed to be attuned to Peronism, but they had no significant impact on the troops or the citizens of Uruguay.

V

The Economy

Because wool and meat are the chief exports of Uruguay, the popular concept of the republic emphasizes its ranching. Montevideo can easily be thought of as government, a maze of bureaus and agencies. But Montevideo also means manufacturing and a commercial tempo. Not only meat-packing plants and textile mills —industries growing out of the nation's agricultural resources— but also plants processing everything from petroleum and cement to alcohol and tires can be found in the Montevidean suburbs.

AGRICULTURE

Sheep and Cattle

In the Uruguayan economy, livestock equates with livelihood. Wool accounts for 53 per cent of the republic's total exports and beef makes up 30 per cent. Together, then, sheep and cattle provide the products for 83 per cent of the nation's annual exports. In terms of the Gross National Product (GNP), ranching and agriculture contribute 17.3 per cent.

In 1900, a livestock census showed that Uruguay contained 18.6 million sheep and 6.8 million cattle; by 1930, those totals had changed to 20.5 million sheep and 7.1 million cattle. In the 1940's and 1950's, high world prices for wool stimulated sheep breeding. In addition, government subsidies for wheat production caused some cattlemen to convert grazing land to agricultural production.

By 1961, Uruguay had 21.5 million sheep and 8.67 million cattle. A 1968 estimate put the totals at 22 million sheep and 8.7 million cattle, or almost three times as many sheep as cattle. During the past twenty years, production of wool has risen 75 per cent, even in the face of lower world prices in the 1960's and the competition of synthetic fibers for some traditional textile markets.

Uruguay's meat exports include not only beef but veal, shipped frozen, chilled, or canned. Six nations of the world account for approximately 70 per cent of the total beef and veal exports on the world market. Uruguay is one of these.

WORLD'S BEEF AND VEAL EXPORTS *(in per cent)*[a]

Country	1952–60 Averages	1964	1965
Australia	16.8	21.4	25.3
Argentina	35.9	25.9	21.4
New Zealand	9.9	8.8	8.1
Uruguay	3.9	7.2	5.1
Netherlands	1.9	4.2	4.4
France	2.7	4.4	3.9
Six-nation total	71.1	71.9	68.2

[a] Compiled by Neal P. Cohen, economist, University of Wisconsin.

Uruguayans consume more meat per capita than the citizens of any other country in the world. Domestic consumption has limited somewhat the sales abroad, but, if cattle and sheep could be brought to slaughter more promptly, Uruguay's foreign earnings could rise sharply.

Ranching Methods

Uruguayan ranchers continue to use traditional methods of raising livestock. As a result, valuable time is lost waiting for steers to reach the suitable weight for slaughtering. The U.S. Department of Agriculture estimates that North American ranchers take from 18 to 21 months to get a steer to its slaughter weight of 450 kilograms, but Uruguayan ranchers take from 52 to 56 months. One result can be seen in this comparison of six large ranching countries.

CATTLE SLAUGHTERED *(as per cent of cattle on ranches)*

Country	1963	1965	1967
United States	34	38	37
Argentina	32	22	23
European Common Market	46	42	43
Australia	32	30	31
New Zealand	40	38	38
Uruguay	17	20	21

SOURCE: U.S. Department of Agriculture, Foreign Agricultural Service.

Uruguay has managed to increase modestly its percentage of slaughtered cattle in terms of its total herds on the ranges. But a briefer fattening-up period would bring weightier cattle to market quicker. Both U.S. and Uruguayan experts estimate that better control of animal diseases and better irrigation to prevent periodic droughts, which deplete grazing lands, would allow Uruguay to double the number of cattle slaughtered each year. One estimate even ventured the hope that Uruguay could quadruple its slaughtered cattle total. World Bank economists report that even moderate improvements in irrigation and disease control have begun to shorten the fattening time for cattle, though traditional methods change slowly.

Sheep-breeding has become more scientific. Sheep are dewormed and dipped against common diseases, and electric power shears have made hand clipping a rarity. The most widely raised breed is the Corriedale, which gives a quality grade of wool desired by textile mills for cloth products. Some carpet wool is also produced.

Dairy Industry

Not only are cattle and sheep grazed together on the same ranches, but in parts of Uruguay beef cattle are raised alongside dairy herds. Before 1930, most Uruguayan cattle were bred for beef, but in that year large numbers of Holstein-Friesian cattle were imported from the Netherlands to make the Uruguayan dairy industry significant in the economy of the republic.

In 1935, the government helped the National Council of Dairy Farmers form a cooperative to buy out the private commercial dairies, incorporating the cooperative society as the *Cooperativa Nacional de Productores de Leche*. (CONAPROLE). The milk producers themselves periodically elect a five-member board of directors, top management for CONAPROLE. With a headquarters in Montevideo, the cooperative maintains its provincial offices in the city of Colonia, in the southwestern part of the republic.

CONAPROLE collects milk from farmers for pasteurization, then delivers milk, butter, and cheese to retail stores. For the city of Montevideo, CONAPROLE has an advantage, for it held a government concession for nine years as a distribution monopoly. Since the end of that period, rival distributors have arisen but cannot match the transportation and organizational facilities of the cooperative.

Ranchers not maintaining their own dairy herds usually buy from small milk retailers in provincial cities. With 80 per cent of all Uruguayans being urban residents, milk distribution in semiurban and rural areas does not constitute a strain on CONAPROLE and other milk retailers.

Farm Crops

Wheat, corn, and flax are the chief farm crops of Uruguay. The republic for much of the 1950's and 1960's was able to supply most of its own domestic needs in these crops and even to yield modest surpluses for export. However, in 1959 and again in 1967 winter floods ruined enough of the wheat crops to force the importing of that grain in modest amounts. On December 20, 1967, the government authorized the Bureau of Agricultural Provisions (*Dirección de Abastecimientos Agropecuarios*) to contract with Argentina for a loan of 70,000 tons of wheat, made necessary by the June and July, 1967, floods in wheat-growing areas of Uruguay.

Almost two decades before, a severe drought had so damaged Uruguayan wheat crops that the government tried to purchase Argentine wheat. But in 1946, the Perón dictatorship in Buenos Aires had little sympathy for the democracy across the Plata estuary and demanded payment in dollars. Thereupon, the United States sent an emergency shipment, earning Uruguayan gratitude and encouraging the Uruguayan wheat producers and the Ministry of Livestockraising and Agriculture to plan for more self-sufficiency in wheat.

From 1947 to 1959, modest increases in wheat crops provided just enough surplus annually to take care of an occasionally flooded crop or a periodic drought-reduced yield. Adverse weather conditions in 1959 and 1960, however, again brought some grain shortages. During the first half of 1960, the United States sold $43 million worth of wheat, corn, barley, cotton, and tobacco to Uruguay, under terms of repayment extending thirty-five years, in pesos, under the U.S. Agricultural Trade Development and Assistance Act.

Then, throughout the 1960's, more acreage went into wheat and other grain production, relieving the pressure on Uruguayan domestic needs whenever flood or drought conditions have arisen, but creating another problem. Some of the pasture lands converted into crop lands should have remained grazing areas in terms of the best interests of the livestock industry. Yet the number of acres involved represent only a relatively small amount of either the pasture or crop lands of the nation.

Truck farming has taken up less than 1 per cent of the Uruguayan land in agricultural use, but in recent decades the yields for vegetable and fruit crops have steadily increased. By 1967 such crops represented almost 20 per cent of all agricultural income. Grapes are grown for domestic and foreign wine companies. Northwestern Uruguay now has a fairly prosperous citrus industry, as orange and lemon producers supply the domestic market.

INDUSTRY

The GNP of $1.5 billion derives from the following sources: 27.3 per cent from manufacturing and construction, 17.3 per cent from farm and ranch production, and 55.4 per cent from transportation, communication, and private and government services. The labor force can be functionally classified as 22 per cent in agriculture and ranching, 27 per cent in manufacturing and construction, and 51 per cent in transportation, communication, finance, electric power and other utilities, personal private services, and government services. Major industries are meat-packing, food-processing, textiles, clothing, bottling plants, and pharmaceuticals. The government owns or controls many of the larger industrial entities through twenty-eight public corporations, resulting in the public sector of the economy accounting for 30 per cent of the GNP.

Many economists have advocated industrialization to free Uruguay of its dependence on foreign markets for its wool, hide, and meat exports. But other economists have opposed too extensive industrialization, pushing instead stepped-up agricultural and livestock production by modern scientific means. A leader of this group, Julio Martínez Lamas, pointing out that the nation's wealth has always been in livestock and crops, contended in a 1946 book that the most natural industries of Uruguay are the food-processing companies and that, as such, they constitute the most appropriate means of enhancing the value of the vital resources of the nation. More than twenty years later, the Martínez Lamas book still had its impact, with deputies and bankers quoting its examples, such as the wool-combing industry being the most appropriate processing field akin to the raising of sheep.

As the early years of the twentieth century brought social and political reforms to Uruguay, economic demands by consumers encouraged a second industrial category, the factories turning out consumer goods that otherwise would have had to be imported at higher prices.

Without large deposits of coal and petroleum, Uruguay has

had to rely on imported fuel and a slowly expanding hydroelectric output. Despite the high cost of bringing fuel into the country to turn the wheels and machinery of factories, by 1967 almost 75 per cent of the manufactured home-consumption goods sold in Uruguay were either produced or assembled in domestic plants.

In 1886, the first electric light plant opened in Montevideo, the first full-scale electric power plant in all of South America. At a time when most Latin American nations clung to gas lamps, Montevideo began installing street lighting and wiring for electricity in private homes. In 1897, the national government acquired the electric power industry from foreign private companies. Today a public or government-owned and -operated corporation, *Usinas Eléctricas y Teléfonos del Estado* (UTE), the State Electric and Telephone Facilities, has a monopoly to supply all electric power service in the country.

For years, imported coal and oil ran the generators that produced the electric current of the republic. The rolling plains of the Banda Oriental are not generally suited for hydroelectric dam projects. Finally, in 1937, in the center of the nation, on the Río Negro, 150 miles north of Montevideo, the first large site was constructed to harness water power into electric power. A dam 3,850 feet wide was completed in 1945, creating the largest artificial lake in South America, the Lago del Río Negro, eighteen miles wide and eighty-seven miles long. A German company, Siemens, began the Río Negro project, but abandoned it because of World War II. Then, a U.S. firm, Westinghouse, completed the hydroelectric complex and connected a transmission line from Rincón del Bonete into Montevideo. Not only electric power, but irrigated farming, flood control, and river navigation followed the completion of this dam project.

In 1956, UTE got a loan from the International Bank for Reconstruction and Development to help build a second hydroelectric project on the Río Negro, fifty-three miles from the Bonete plant at Rincón de Baygorría. The additional power helped run a new sugar refinery, several fertilizer plants, four paper factories, a leather tannery, and a new cement plant that had been awaiting new sources of electricity.

As Uruguay looks to the 1970's and 1980's, her government economists urge consideration of an ambitious plan by the United Nations to build an international hydroelectric complex to benefit the entire Río de la Plata Basin. On June 26, 1967, the Inter-American Development Bank made a grant of $250,000 for a preliminary study for a multinational water-resources plan for the region from Argentina to southern Brazil. In September, 1963, Ambassador Carlos Salamanca, regional director of the U.N. office in Montevideo, formally announced his Plata project in a forty-five–page preliminary study. Salamanca pointed out that the basin of the region is fed by the Paraná, Paraguay, Uruguay, and Plata rivers, with valuable waters of this basin spilling into the Atlantic Ocean.

A joint development of the basin has long been a dream of the leaders of the five countries through which these waters flow— Argentina, Brazil, Bolivia, Paraguay, and Uruguay. When the presidents of the hemisphere under the auspices of the Organization of American States (OAS) held a summit meeting at Punta del Este, Uruguay, in April, 1967, this "Proyecto de la Cuenca de la Plata" received some attention. By the end of 1967, OAS survey teams were drawing up detailed reports for the full-scale development of the regional waterways for more electricity, more flood control, and more irrigated farming. Even though it will be 1975 before the first concrete gets poured, the Plata Basin project promises Uruguay enough electric power at reasonable rates for full-scale industrialization, should its national leaders push the economy in that direction. In 1968 the detailed preliminary plans seemed merely small beginnings, but they were a significant drop in the basin.

A government corporation, the *Administración Nacional de Combustibles, Alcohol y Portland* (ANCAP), the National Administration of Fuels, Alcohol, and Cement, imports much crude oil and has a monopoly on refining it. At its La Teja refinery, built in 1961, near Montevideo, one of South America's most modern plants for petroleum products, ANCAP produces more than 8,000 cubic meters of high-octane gasoline daily.

Meat-Packing Industry

With sufficient refined fuel and electric power to run modern refrigeration plants, Uruguay is one of the world's important meat-packers. In prerefrigeration years, the vast quantities of meat and mutton being raised had to be salted and dried. By the 1860's, chemical extracts had improved the preservation of jerked beef enough to make Uruguay an important supplier of European dinner tables.

Food-processing industries remain economically the most important industrial group in Uruguay, with meat-packing the biggest enterprise of this category. In fact, a meat-processing plant launched modern industry in the republic. In the city of Fray Bentos, on the Uruguay River, in 1865 the Liebig Meat Extract Company of London began manufacturing meat extract. By 1871 that factory was producing annually 6 million pounds of jerked beef and 571,000 pounds of meat extract. Then, in 1904, the Uruguayan meat industry modernized and introduced refrigeration plants for frozen and chilled meat called *frigoríficos*. Four huge *frigoríficos* at Fray Bentos still account for 95 per cent of the national output of processed meat.

In 1928 the government established the Frigorífico Nacional (commonly called Frigonal) , to compete with the privately owned plants that concentrated on export trade. Frigonal has been concerned with the domestic market as well as exports. By 1957, the two large foreign-owned meat-packers, Swift and Armour, could no longer make a profit. They had to compete for cattle and sheep with Frigonal, whose governmental subsidies permitted it to pay higher prices. Labor disputes added to the shortage of slaughter animals, and Swift and Armour ended operations.

In 1958, a cooperative society of employees, Meat-Packing Establishments of the Cerro (*Establecimientos Frigoríficos del*

Cerro), acquired the Swift and Armour facilities. The legislature appropriated funds so that the new co-op would enjoy tax exemptions, a period of free rent, and a ten-year loan of 5.6 million pesos at 5 per cent interest.

In 1967, the British-owned meat-packing plant, Anglo, at Fray Bentos, closed down and in 1968 was converted into another cooperative run by Uruguayan employees. Various other small meat-packers exist in provincial Uruguay, several of them just beyond the city limits of Montevideo, for, by law, Frigonal has a monopoly for the slaughter of cattle and sheep inside Montevideo.

Since 1959, however, Frigonal has been permitted, under a "free supply" law, to allow smaller packers to utilize its facilities for a fee during slack hours. More than thirty private companies make use of this service. One such company, Cattivelli Brothers, can keep its restaurants and retail butcher shops adequately supplied with meat by using Frigonal facilities. And, on a bus heading northeast on Camino Maldonado, toward the town of Piedras Blancas, for example, one can see women with market baskets headed for branches of the Cattivelli *frigorífico*, where they can buy the same quality of meat as Frigonal offers at lower prices.

Frigonal's board of directors has five members, with one member being nominated by the national government, one by the municipal government of Montevideo, one by the Ministry of the Interior, and two by the livestock producer associations *Asociación Rural* and *Federación Rural*.

New meat-packing plants have opened in provincial areas closer to ranching suppliers of animals. For instance, *Indagro*, a company owned by U. S. and Uruguayan investors, operates plants in Rocha and San Carlos. And secondary industries have grown up near meat-packing plants. Trucks haul the slaughtered waste products to these firms, which make glue and fertilizer.

Textiles

Almost the entire Uruguayan textile industry is located in Montevideo. With wool being the chief resource of the nation, textiles can be considered to constitute the most important urban industry in the republic. All wool used in the weaving of cloth and blankets and in combing and spinning into yarn is domestic, but the machinery in the mills is imported. The principal woolen firm of the nation, La Nacional, is a private company owned by the Campomar y Soulas corporation. For almost a century, La Nacional has set the pace for Uruguayan weaving.

Campomar y Soulas also operates the largest cotton mill in Uruguay, the Primera Hilandería. Second largest cotton mill is the Alpargatas, an affiliate of the Argentine company of the same name. These two mills together produce one-third of the domestic requirements for cotton textiles. The cotton itself is imported from Paraguay and from the United States.

Rayon and other synthetic fibers are used more and more in the smaller and newer textile mills in Montevideo. Tailor shops and clothing manufacturers find that Uruguayan worsteds are of very good quality, but a popular concept puts a snobbish value on British worsted fabrics for high-priced suits. In the late 1960's, Uruguayan woolen products were beginning to hold their own in terms of fashion with British imports in both men's and women's clothing.

ANCAP

The largest importer in Uruguay is the government corporation ANCAP, which imports crude oil and has a monopoly on refining it. ANCAP operates its own retail service stations and acts as wholesale distributor for gasoline for the three competing private foreign companies—Shell, Standard, and Texaco—that offer the same retail prices as ANCAP stations. Standard and Shell have the largest number of service stations in Montevideo, but in some of the smaller provincial cities only ANCAP outlets are to be found.

ANCAP's largest cement plant is at Minas, sixty-two miles east of the capital. In November, 1967, the Inter-American Development Bank made a loan of $6 million to build a new cement plant at Paysandú, with a capacity of 100,000 metric tons a year, anticipating a doubled output in the 1970's. Alliance for Progress economists have called ANCAP's cement division one of the better-run public enterprises in Latin America.

Limestone deposits at Quequay, near Paysandú, are extensive enough to guarantee ANCAP sufficient reserves to supply its cement plants with clay for the next ninety years. Storage and packaging facilities for cement are modern and efficient, assuring good nationwide distribution and dockside growth as production expands. In 1971, cement production will rise to 800,000 metric tons, with customers already on a waiting list in Paraguay and Argentina. ANCAP operates its own fleet of barges and tankers to move petroleum and cement from Montevideo to the river ports of Salto and Paysandú.

ANCAP manufactures not only industrial and medical alcohol, but also the type that goes into fermented drinks for human consumption. ANCAP whisky and cognac are marketed in taverns and retail stores all over Uruguay.

Tire Companies

The Uruguayan Tire Factory, *Fábrica Uruguaya de Neumáticos* (FUNSA), was established in the late 1930's with the technical help of the Goodrich Rubber Company of the United States. FUNSA was granted a nine-year monopoly to manufacture rubber tires for automobiles, trucks, motorcycles, and bicycles. Under the 1952 and 1966 constitutions, the General Assembly has the authority to encourage new, vital industries by offering nine-year monopolies. Thus, when FUNSA's monopoly period ended, a rival private firm, the E. Ghiringhelli Company, known as EGSA, began its production, but by the late 1940's the domestic market for rubber goods had grown large enough to absorb the output of both companies. FUNSA also makes rubber tubes, tennis shoes, rubber boots, raincoats, rubber rafts and boats, rubber gloves, and various other products used in sports and recreation.

EGSA, with technical assistance from the Akron Tire Company of Ohio, manufactures a Uruguayan equivalent of the Mohawk brand of tire. Both FUNSA and EGSA tire products have been of such good quality that Argentine racing drivers regularly journey from Buenos Aires to Montevideo to buy special tires for high-speed racers.

TRANSPORTATION

Although more than half of the population of Uruguay lives in, or adjacent to, the national capital, the remaining 1.3 million Uruguayans have no difficulty staying in communication with Montevideo. The network of highways allows a steady flow of automobiles, trucks, and buses to and from the national capital. All roads lead to Montevideo, but, in the sense of national social and economic integration, all roads also lead away to the other cities of the republic.

Unlike almost all other Latin American nations, Uruguay has no high mountain ranges, which make highway construction exorbitant and painfully slow. No town of any consequence in the nation remains isolated from Montevideo by road. Main highways are paved, and minor roads are gravel-topped but level. Trucks and buses move freight and passengers around the republic rapidly and inexpensively.

Numerous garages dot the neighborhoods of Montevideo and the principal provincial cities. With the highest-grade gasoline in Latin America — with the exception of Venezuela — Uruguay can remain on wheels, even with the high import taxes on automobiles. With high-octane fuel and low-cost mechanics, Uruguayans seem to drive automobiles forever. The avenues of Montevideo abound with 1946 Fords, 1939 Chevrolets, and vintage Renaults and Triumphs. A connoisseur of antique automobiles should visit the beaches of Pocitos Malvín, Buceo in the Montevidean suburbs, or Rodó and Batlle parks to see Model T Fords, 1930 Buicks, and other models long out of manufacture, ranging from Packards to Hupmobiles.

The *Organización Nacional de Autotransportes* (ONDA) is the national intercity bus company, a private corporation with Greyhound Bus vehicles. Within Montevideo, both public and private companies compete in offering city bus service.

Railroads

During the decade of the 1860's, railroads connected the republic's most remote towns with Montevideo. By 1911, a British company had completed the network of tracks in essentially their present form, giving Uruguay a greater railroad mileage in proportion to its total land area than that of any other nation in the Western Hemisphere, including the United States.

Gradually, government lines fed into the British-owned Central Uruguayan Railroad system. On January 31, 1949, the Minister of Public Works, Manuel Rodríguez Correa, in an elaborate ceremony at the Montevideo railroad station, formally turned over to the President of the Republic, Luis Batlle Berres, the Central Railroad, the legislature previously having appropriated the funds to buy out the British company. Thus, another public corporation, the *Administración de los Ferrocarriles del Estado* (AFE), the Administration of State Railroads, began operating all passenger and freight trains of the nation.

Airplanes and Ships

One national airline, *Primeras Líneas Uruguayas de Navegación*, began in 1936 as a private company, becoming a government corporation in 1944. A competing domestic airline, CAUSA, privately owned, began operations in 1938 but closed down in May, 1967, although investors who bought it from bankruptcy receivers plan to revive it in 1970. Fifteen foreign airlines connect Montevideo's international airport, Carrasco, with the major cities of the world.

Similarly, Montevideo's port facilities host the steamships and freighters of the major maritime nations of the world, linking Montevideo with ports around the globe. The regular Uruguayan merchant marine fleet, exclusive of the ANCAP-owned fleet, has eleven merchant ships and three tankers. Of 1,600 ocean-going vessels that dock annually at Montevideo, only fourteen vessels with a gross tonnage of 103,000 fly the Uruguayan flag. Montevideo is also the winter anchorage of the Antarctic whaling flotillas and the only port of call on the South American mainland for ships going to and from the Falkland Islands.

Municipal Transportation

Tens of thousands of workers in the public and private corporations and in the retail companies in greater Montevideo shuttle back and forth to work on buses. The social custom of a siesta, or midday break from work, not only for a meal but as a rest period means that Montevideo really has four traffic peaks a day. Private automobiles abound and buses become crowded not only at the opening hour in the morning and at closing time in late afternoon or early evening, but also during the times when workers go home to eat a noon meal and when they return to offices and factories.

With hundreds of restaurants with quality food at relatively reasonable prices, not only downtown Montevideo but every suburb of the capital manages to hold a majority of its employees within a few blocks of their places of employment. But transportation officials for the capital estimate that 40-45 per cent of all workers still make the extra two bus trips a day to get home for lunch.

From the turn of the century to the end of World War II, a British company owned and operated streetcars. In 1947 this foreign tramway company was purchased by the municipal government of Montevideo, and the streetcars or trams were replaced with electric buses. The trolley-buses cover the same routes that the electric streetcars did, in order to follow the overhead lines that supply power, but the tracks have all been removed, giving buses more flexibility in traffic. The British tramway company had not been making a profit and the extensive replacement of equipment needed in 1947 encouraged the municipal transportation corporation to change from electric streetcars to buses.

In 1947 the legislature created the Municipal Transportation Administration, *Administración Municipal de Transportes* (AMDET), not as the holder of a monopoly on city transportation but merely as one of the two major Montevideo transportation systems. Competing with AMDET is the privately owned Uruguayan Transportation Company. Only AMDET maintains trolley-buses, but both companies operate standard gasoline-engine buses over every neighborhood in metropolitan Montevideo. In addition, a smaller bus line serves streets not covered by the two major companies. Not a neighborhood in Montevideo or its surrounding suburbs lacks frequent bus schedules from before dawn to past midnight. On major avenues and boulevards, if a gray AMDET bus has been missed, the passenger will wait not more than ten minutes before a blue private bus comes along.

The distance from the Plaza de Independenzia and the Plaza Libertad in the heart of downtown Montevideo to suburban Carrasco can be traveled in less than one hour, except for peak periods of traffic, when one hour and forty-five minutes is required to go from the heart of the city to the fashionable suburb ten miles away.

Before the severe inflation of the 1960's, AMDET kept fares very low, forcing the rival companies into line. In July, 1951, the voters of Montevideo actually held a plebiscite to decide whether municipal fares should be raised a few pennies to allow salary raises and expansion of the transportation system. This referendum was the first of its kind in the history of Uruguay, hailed as a healthy example of "direct democracy in action" by the newspapers. A clause in the older constitutions and in the 1966 constitution provides that, if one-fifth of the total voting population of a department or of the republic appeals against any measure taken to increase public expenditure, then a plebiscite may be held to decide the issue. In the 1951 election, the proposed increase in municipal fares was decisively rejected. By contrast, in 1967, under severe inflationary pressures, both major bus lines agreed to raise fares, evoking some public protest but no hint of any plebiscite.

Taxicabs in Montevideo have meters, but, with the inflation of the 1960's, some drivers use a chart because their meters have to be adjusted to higher rates approximately every six months. Taxi fares have remained relatively low, with government subsidies to the private companies making up annual budgetary deficits. All Montevideo taxis are painted black, with a lighted sign above the meter letting the potential customer know if the taxi is engaged or free. Taxis can be summoned by telephone, but most permanent residents of Montevideo usually get a cab by walking to the nearest taxi stand, which is never more than four or five blocks away from any part of the downtown area, though they are relatively far apart in the suburbs.

All in all, the big-city tempo of Montevideo throbs with a crowded public transportation system, but one that provides buses and taxis at most places at most hours of the day or night.

VI

People and Society

Uruguayans are European in origin, the few Indians having been killed off or driven into Paraguay when the Spaniards and Portuguese came in the sixteenth century. In addition to Spanish and Portuguese surnames, which predominate, almost one-fourth of Uruguayan surnames are Italian or Hispanicized from Italian. Less than 1 per cent of the population is Negro, mostly grandchildren of Brazilians who moved southward. Uruguay therefore escapes the internal colonialism that plagues many Latin American nations, for no ethnically European elite presides over the exploitation of Indians and mestizos.

Nor does an urban minority economically oppress a downtrodden rural majority. Uruguayans are overwhelmingly middleclass urbanites, yet a distinction must be made between city and country folk. Uruguay has one of the highest urbanization rates in the world, with 44.6 per cent of all Uruguayans living in Montevideo and 61.2 per cent of the nation's people living in cities of more than 20,000. Thus, a Uruguayan is a big-city bureaucrat, bank clerk, teacher, student, shopkeeper. But he is also a ranch hand, farmer, fisherman, meat-packer, truckdriver. And, in the capital or the provincial towns, he is a politician, newspaper reader, radio-television listener, and a joiner. He or she belongs to a club and to any number of political, civic, trade, or professional groups. A Uruguayan pauses often to sip tea, and he does so in public with his friends.

UNIFORMS ARE ACADEMIC SMOCKS

Civilian-dominated Uruguay sports few military uniforms even near defense and naval installations in Montevideo. The most common uniform in Uruguay is the school smock, worn by primary-school students over their regular clothes to give poor children equal status with wealthier classmates and to promote school spirit.

In the heart of downtown Montevideo, however, one bit of pageantry has military overtones. The elite guard on duty at the offices of the president of the republic come from the cavalry regiment with the best record of barracks efficiency and good deportment. Presidential guards at Government House must wear dress uniforms of dark blue with red trimmings and topped with busby dress hats and cavalry swords, the one bit of ceremonial splendor democratic Uruguay allows its chief executives. Similarly, the top-ranking infantry regiment, in white and green dress uniforms and blue shakos, performs the ceremonial guard duty at the Supreme Court. But, at the legislature, only policemen are on guard duty.

In contrast to all other Latin American nations, Uruguay does not have an elaborate presidential palace. Rather, it maintains a neat but modest *Casa de Gobierno,* or Government House, facing the Plaza de Independencia in the heart of Montevideo, with various cabinet ministries scattered throughout the central sector of the city. On the other hand, the *Palacio Legislativo,* or Legislative Palace, is large and ornate, emphasizing architecturally the vigorous representative government.

The Legislative Palace dominates the broad Agraciada Avenue from a knoll. Inaugurated in 1925, it was designed by the distinguished Italian architect Gaetano Moretti. Its granite and marble hallways and spacious chambers cost $12 million. Forty-five varieties of marble from various parts of the republic combine into artistic mosaic floors and walls. Stained-glass windows and historic paintings make the building an attraction not only for tourists but also for Uruguayans. Lobbyists from provincial towns, capital residents speaking for organized interests, and numerous government functionaries mingle in the Legislative Palace. They usually are dressed formally but chat in a casual manner.

RELIGION

In terms of religious affiliation, Uruguay somewhat approaches, proportionately, the pluralism of U.S. society. Unlike the other Latin American republics, which list formal Roman Catholic affiliations of 90–95 per cent, Uruguay as early as its 1908 census counted only 61 per cent of its population Catholic. Its 1963 census indicates that almost the same proportion, 62 per cent, claim formal affiliation with the Catholic Church.

In recent decades, Uruguay has become a stronghold of Protestantism in Latin America. In Montevideo, Paysandú, Salto, Rivera, and Artigas, active congregations support forty-two large Methodist Churches, plus forty Mormon, thirty-nine Baptist, and thirty-seven Lutheran churches, as well as smaller numbers of Seventh Day Adventists, Presbyterians, Episcopalians, and Waldensians. Three Christian Science societies serve large congregations in Montevideo, supporting a 1,000-seat, block-square church, plus a busy downtown reading room.

Six synagogues in Montevideo serve Jewish congregations larger in size than many of their counterparts in the United States. The *Congregación Sefaradi* in 1932 built a large temple to serve hundreds of Jews with Spanish and Portuguese surnames, who trace their ancestry back to the Iberian peninsula, to Holland and North Africa, and thence to South America. An atmosphere of religious and political freedom in the 1930's attracted Jews from Germany to Uruguay, though an earlier wave of immigration at the turn of the century paralleled one of the big influxes of Italian immigration.

The late Horacio Asiaín Márquez, distinguished newspaper columnist for the daily *El Debate*, in 1956 established the Confraternidad Judía-Cristiana del Uruguay (Jewish-Christian Fraternal Order of Uruguay), Latin America's only counterpart of the U.S. National Conference of Christians and Jews, a symbol of the climate of brotherhood in which Uruguayan democracy has flourished. The Asiaín Márquez family, prominent in lay Catholic circles, includes Jesuit priests and diplomats among Uruguay's national leaders.

Separation of Church and state came peacefully in 1919, but even under the longtime 1830 constitution, which remained in force until then, other faiths were tolerated, though officially the government had supported the Roman Catholic Church. Such toleration in nineteenth-century Latin America was rare. In 1844, the British merchants, whose fathers had come to Montevideo in 1807 and remained after their troops withdrew, built Trinity Church to serve Anglicans, one of the first Protestant churches built in Latin America with government approval. When a new sea wall was constructed along the Montevideo waterfront in 1935, the historic English church was moved stone by stone several hundred yards inland, with the full cooperation of the national government, which valued its significance as a Uruguayan historical landmark.

Though the Uruguayan Government remains vigorously secular, it appropriated funds in 1967 to help refurbish the outside walls of the Cathedral of Montevideo, because this Catholic site held historical significance for the nation.

The Roman Catholic Church

During the decades of growing secularization of Uruguayan society, since the 1890's, the Roman Catholic Church did not exert much political power. When the constitution of 1919 peacefully separated Church and state, Catholic lay leaders raised an endowment fund of $1 million to compensate for the loss of government subsidies. The constitutions of 1934, 1952, and 1966 did not alter the 1919 provisions concerning religion. Uruguayans are free to practice all faiths, and the Catholic Church retains its properties tax free. To emphasize the separation of Church and state, Uruguay is the only Latin American republic to designate Christmas as "Family Day" and Holy Week preceding Easter Sunday as "Tourist Week," or sometimes *Semana Criolla,* emphasizing colonial gaucho traditions.

Aside from its longtime political activity in the Civic Union, which is now the Christian Democratic Party, the Catholic Church of Uruguay has lent itself mostly to things spiritual and social. Around 1900, the Catholic Workers' Circle was organized, and in the 1960's a few Catholic labor unions have been active.

No famous Catholic shrine exists in Uruguay, nor does the nation have any widely recognized patron saint, on the order of the Virgin of Guadalupe of Mexico. The pilgrimage to the statue of the Miraculous Virgin atop Verdún Hill near the city of Minas is the only religious procession at all echoing the institutionalized public pilgrimages found in most predominantly Catholic countries. Basically, Church prelates and Catholic lay leaders speak through the Christian Democratic Party or through some factions of the National Party. A few conservative Blancos on occasion lend their efforts to programs considered essentially Catholic.

LABOR UNIONS

The first Uruguayan labor unions were founded in 1895, organized by European immigrants who followed either the political philosophy of the socialists or the anarchists. At that time, the government of Uruguay had no sympathy for organized labor. That attitude changed, however, when José Batlle y Ordóñez became president of the republic in 1903. Batlle's sympathy for labor culminated in his signing into law on November 17, 1915, the first statute in all of Latin America establishing an eight-hour workday in industry.

As late as 1929, the number of union members in Uruguay totaled only 25,000, but in the economic depression of the 1930's the ranks of labor began to swell. Modern trade-union organization began in 1940, when the *Unión General de Trabajadores*

(UGT), or General Workers Union, brought together 40,000 members from thirty-one individual unions. Drawn principally from the construction, maritime, textile, transportation, and service industries, the UGT found that Uruguay's extensive social legislation had robbed the federation of many of the talking points that trade unions could champion in other Latin American nations.

Communists began to infiltrate the UGT almost from its inception. One of the UGT's first demands was that the government establish diplomatic relations with the Soviet Union. Enrique Rodríguez, who was elected a senator in 1966 and had previously been a deputy representing first the Communist Party and then FIdeL, in the 1950's as secretary-general of the UGT carried the labor federation deeper into Communist programs. As publisher of the Communist daily newspaper, *El Popular,* in the early 1960's Rodríguez was encouraging newer labor groups to emulate the UGT.

In November, 1959, the UGT announced that it was Communist-led and Communist-oriented. Because of disenchantment with the Communist aura of the UGT, a second labor federation, the *Confederación General de Trabajo* (CGT), began to grow in the 1950's. But the CGT also leaned toward authoritarianism, especially right-wing Peronism from neighboring Argentina. At its peak, the CGT had no more than 3,500 members, compared to approximately 35,000 in the UGT in the early 1950's.

Democratic trade unionists who rejected both Communism and Peronism began to support a third labor federation, the *Confederación Sindical del Uruguay* (CSU). By 1956, the CSU had become the strongest and largest Uruguayan labor federation, but after 1958 began to decline as its members were lured into the *Central Unica de Trabajadores* (CUT), which the Communists had encouraged as the principal labor federation after their own UGT had begun to falter.

In the 1960's, inflation gave unions a continuing reason to strike for higher pay. Whenever the government attempted even modest austerity programs to halt inflation, union dissatisfaction asserted itself not only in strikes but in political maneuvers among the left-wing elements in the political parties.

In 1952, anti-Communist forces in the bus drivers union began their struggle against the UGT leadership. When one of the anti-Communist bus leaders was killed, these unions withdrew from the UGT, with other unions following. Today, drivers for city buses of all three municipal companies belong to the Autonomous Union of Bus Drivers (*Sindicato Autónomo del Omnibus*), an affiliate of the Federation of Uruguayan Transport Workers, which includes the unions of drivers of intercity and provincial bus lines, as well as workers of the Port of Montevideo, ranging from stevedores to seamen of the merchant marines. Neither railroad nor aviation workers unions have shown any inclination to form any national transportation federation, however.

By 1954 the UGT had shrunk from 50,000 to 15,000 members. Reflecting this decline, the Communist Party lost its seat in the Senate and three seats in the Chamber of Deputies in 1954. Without a vigorous organized labor reserve, the Communists could not hang on to their elected legislative beachhead. But by the 1960's the Communist alliance, the FIdeL, had regained the lost electoral strength and in the 1966 election did better than ever in terms of total votes and seats in the legislature.

In 1962, the CUT, with a membership of 50,000, had replaced the defunct UGT but retained some of the same UGT Communist leaders. By 1967, it had built its membership to 290,000, again under a new label, *Convención Nacional de Trabajadores* (CNT), or National Workers Convention. Its anti-Communist rival, the CSU, by 1962 had 71,000 members, but by 1967 had a declining membership of 10,000. Other non-CNT groups are: the Uruguayan Trade Union Action, with a membership of 5,000, oriented toward the Christian Democratic Party; the Federation of Uruguayan Transport Workers, with a membership of 3,000; and the Regional Workers Federation of Uruguay, with 2,500 members.

Two civil-servant unions loosely tied to the CNT, the *Con-*

federación de Organizaciones de Funcionarios del Estado (Federation of Civil Servant Organizations) and the *Mesa Sindical Coordinadora* (Coordinating Trade Union Roundtable) — the latter speaks for the employees of autonomous entities and decentralized services, such as the railroads and the telephone service — represent workers in government and public corporations, the major employers of the nation, with payrolls larger than individual private industries.

In the 1960's, more than 300,000 Uruguayans were affiliated with trade unions. In 1961, the Communist Party admitted that its membership totaled only 13,241. Within the ranks of organized labor, not three union members in 100 were Communists, yet among officials of fourteen key unions, eight out of ten strategic posts were held by Communists.

Communist Party Secretary Rodney Arismendi, a deputy in the Chamber of Representatives, has asserted that "the vehicle of the ascendency of Communists will be the united workers of this land, trade unionists." In Uruguay, Communist officials in unions foment strikes for any excuse in order to cripple the Uruguayan economy and create government chaos, engendering a power vacuum to be filled by Communists. If partial work stoppages are included, Uruguay has been suffering more than 700 strikes annually in recent years. Arismendi stated at a conference in Moscow that "In a single year, I have fomented eighty-two strikes." The problem that Uruguayan trade unions have of ridding themselves of Communist officials remains a principal headache for both labor and management.

CIVIL SERVICE

With the public corporations and decentralized services added to the executive, legislative, and judicial branches of government, a large proportion of Uruguay's work force is employed by the state, although many are engaged in activities as varied as railroading and alcohol production. Numerous boards and commissions regulate rents, control prices, and oversee tourist facilities.

URUGUAY

Scale of Miles

0   20   40   60

ARGENTINA

Bella Unión
Artigas
Cuareim River
CUCHILLA DE STA. ANA
B R A Z I L

ARTIGAS

CUCHILLA DE BELÉN
Rivera
Livramento

Concordia
Salto

SALTO

RIVERA
Minas de Corrales
Bagé

Tacuarembó

Uruguay River

PAYSANDÚ

Tacuarembó
TACUAREMBÓ

Yaguarón R.

Paysandú

CUCHILLA DE HAEDO

River

Melo

Concepción del Uruguay

RÍO
Paso de los Toros

NEGRO

RINCON DEL BONETE

Río Negro Reservoir

CERRO LARGO

Rio Branco

Negro

Yi

DURAZNO

Durazno River

Vergara

TREINTA Y TRES

Treinta y Tres

Fray Bentos

Mercedes

Trinidad

SORIANO

FLORES

Sarandí Grande

Laguna Mirim

Carmelo

COLONIA

SAN

San José de Mayo

FLORIDA

Florida

LA CUCHILLA GRANDE

Cebollatí

ROCHA

Chuy

Colonia

JOSÉ

San Ramón

Minas

Rocha

MALDONADO
San Carlos

Puerto La Paloma

Río de la Plata

Buenos Aires

La Plata

Canelones

CANELONES

MONTEVIDEO
Montevideo

Piriápolis
Carrasco

Maldonado
Punta del Este
Lobos I.

ARGENTINA

A T L A N T I C
O C E A N

José Gervasio Artigas (1764–1850), "father of Uruguayan independence," led the revolutionary struggle to free Uruguay from control by Brazil and Argentina. (Detail from a fresco by Fernando Leal in the Bolivar Amphitheater of Mexico's National University.)

José Batlle y Ordóñez (1856–1929), "father of modern Uruguay," was the distinguished statesman who initiated much of the important social legislation incorporated in his country's constitution. *Ministry of Tourism, Uruguay*

The modern Hospital de Clinicas is a fine example of the strides Uruguay has taken in the area of public health. Much emphasis is placed on preventive medicine, and free medical care is available for all who are unable to pay.

The main square of San José, like those in most Uruguayan towns, provides a focus for the life of the town. *J. Allan Cash—Rapho Guillumette*

Gauchos round up one of the many herds of sheep that provide the country with two of its most valuable commodities—mutton and wool. *Authenticated News International*

A colony of seals basks in the sun on the rocky coast of Lobos Island, near Punta del Este. Each season, more than 30,000 seals breed here, supplying exporters with large amounts of fur and leather. *Government of Uruguay*

Cattle are big business in Uruguay, where most of gauchos round up a herd in Rivera, on the Bra-

Uruguay has more sheep and cattle in proportion to land area than any other Latin American country. Production costs are low, and the quality of the product is high. *J. Allan Cash—Rapho Guillumette*

Lush fields of flowering linseed enhance the landscape of upcountry farms. *J. Allan Cash—Rapho Guillumette*

Punta del Este, an international resort city near Montevideo, is a traditional site for meetings of the Organization of American States, the Alliance for Progress, and the Latin American Free Trade Association. *Pan American*

The graceful sweep of Pocitos Beach, the most popular in the Montevideo area, attracts Uruguayans and tourists alike.

Even the famed hotel gambling casinos of Montevideo are part of the government.

With strong tenure rights through civil service statutes and through labor-union contracts, Uruguayan civil servants are not easily discharged, even for inefficiency. A proliferating bureaucracy has resulted in delays in the expediting of even the most basic government functions.

Take, for example, the processing of pensions for retiring civil servants, something that presumably even the government employees handling the paper work would hold in esteem in terms of potential self-interest. Often several months go by as quadruplicate sets of papers are shuffled back and forth. As one pension-office expert put it, "If I could reduce my work force 20 per cent, I could speed up pension payments to where paper work would be finalized in half the time." Even allowing for exaggeration, this comment does typify the remarks gathered in government offices by conscientious investigators for President Pacheco's 1968 study of the problem.

On the positive side, citizens know that the public administrators are selected by a government itself genuinely representative of the citizenry, chosen in honest and open elections. A Uruguayan may criticize the proliferating bureaucracy, but he feels pride in knowing that he helped vote the government into power and that he is free to organize opposition to it and to campaign for its defeat, modification, or continuation. If the citizen cannot exert enough pressure on his own, he has his political party faction and other organized interest groups, ranging from professional to trade and from social to economic.

Bureaucrats at Work and Play

In the government offices of Montevideo and the departmental capitals, an army of civil servants shuffles papers. In the business divisions of public corporations, a second set of government employees presides over state-owned and -operated utilities and decentralized services. Men in gray business suits and women in stylish frocks people desks far out of proportion to the actual operations of the entities to which they are assigned. Regardless of official schedules, many government clerks and minor administrators work a half day. In the summer, office time may be mornings, so that afternoons can be spent at the beach; in the winter, office time may be afternoons, so that chilly mornings can be spent at home.

For those bureaucrats who work a day-long shift, and for tens of thousands of workers in factories and private stores all over Montevideo, late afternoon means a pause similar to the coffee break of their U.S. counterparts. At tea time, urban workers seek out the nearest *confitería,* or snack shop, where a cup of tea and a sandwich punctuate a brief rest period.

In conversations at tea time, the true tempo of the big city can be heard in terms of Uruguayan attitudes. What are people talking about, worrying about, embracing as current fads? Words streaming from the tea salons become verbal calipers, measuring one social dimension of the republic's culture. In a sense, the Montevideo *confitería* is a social equalizer. For example, the sandwich shop for workers from the Andrés Deus building-block factory on Carrasco Road frequently also plays host to wealthy matrons pausing between a downtown shopping tour and their suburban Carrasco residences.

Going from the old business sector of Montevideo toward the fashionable beaches, driving along the Rambla, or sea-wall avenue facing the harbor, one passes low-rent public housing units built by the government National Low-Cost Housing Institute, or *Instituto Nacional de Viviendas Económicas* (INVE), established in 1937 as an administrative dependency of the Ministry of Public Works. Residents of INVE apartments can be found sipping tea in salons in nearby business neighborhoods, where managers of retail stores and junior executives from the branches of the sixty-four private commercial banks and from the large government banks also pause in their afternoon's work.

Families in middle- and upper-income brackets tend to buy

homes or rent apartments in the suburbs. However, in the past couple of decades, more of these families have purchased their own apartments in condominium buildings, a trend that began in 1946 with the promulgation of a law on cooperative ownership of buildings. Luxury-class condominiums are located on Larrañaga Avenue, near the Buceo beach and yacht club. But less deluxe types can be found near the older business sections, where residents patronize the same nearby tea salons frequented by factory and office workers.

Along 18 de Julio Avenue and Agraciada Avenue, hundreds and hundreds of clerical workers also take time for tea. But the employees of the Ministry of the Interior are not likely to encounter those from the Ministry of Defense, for the various entities of government are scattered throughout Montevideo, few of them near enough to each other to constitute a cluster.

GAUCHOS

A ranch hand at work does not fit closely the stereotype sought by a tourist with a camera. He often wears denim work jeans similar to North American Levis, more so than the baggy riding pants of gaucho tradition. A soft black hat, with a small brim that turns up in front to meet the breezes wafting across the pampa, serves in place of the broad-brimmed hat of the western ranges of the United States and Canada and the even broader-brimmed hats of the *vaqueros* of Mexico.

In the nineteenth century, the classical gaucho roamed the flat ranges of the Banda Oriental, but he was a cowboy or sheepman working ranges that were unfenced. Unlike his modern counterpart, he did not consistently have to wield wirecutters and pliers. As historian Thomas F. McGann has observed, ranching was esteemed because it often was "synonymous with dominion over the largest extents of land, and because it was farther removed from farming, from grubbing in the soil."

This cowboy-sheepman-horseman was the dominant figure of the "Age of Leather," a period from the Spanish colonial days through the 1890's, when leather thongs, saddles, hides, and meat were indispensable to the daily lives of Uruguayans. With the pampa flat and devoid of mountains, a gaucho needed to stand in his saddle to view the horizon, and that meant soft boots, instead of the hard, high-heeled variety that his North American counterpart developed. Even today soft boots are widely used.

An all-purpose blanket with an opening stitched in the center served as an overcoat, raincoat, pillow, and blanket. Today, when sleeping accommodations even in the remotest corners of Uruguay mean a bed indoors for the ranch hands, the poncho has lost its blanket use of yesteryear and has become more tailored, fancier in color, and more specialized as a topcoat. Ranch and farm workers still wear what can be recognized as gaucho-style garments, but these clothes have been modified by sewing machine and synthetic fabric additions.

Meat is still the ranch workers' chief food, but the consumption of vegetables has increased. *Yerba maté,* a tea brewed from the leaves of an indigenous holly, as in centuries past, remains the principal drink of the rural Uruguayan. Supplementing his dried gourd as a container, today's ranch hand keeps his supply of tea hot in a thermos bottle purchased in town. He blends tradition with modern living, putting his *bombilla,* or silver-coated metal straw, into his manufactured thermos bottle.

Similarly, the traditional sheepskins still serve as a base for the rancher's saddle, but something new has been added: a transistor radio, bringing him news and music while he rides the range. In the smaller towns of Uruguay, one can still see the traditional gaucho saddle, or *recado.* It consists of *sudaderas,* or sweatcloths, on top of which come *mandiles,* or colored wool layers, topped in turn by a *carona,* or leather. Over the entire pile of coverings rests the *cojinillo,* a sheepskin with the wool side up, and a *sobrepuesto,* or final leather covering. A majority of modern Uruguayan horsemen, however, use saddles similar to those found in the western United States, with the colorful *recado* reserved for annual festivals or carnival celebrations. With the adoption of modern saddles, most Uruguayan horsemen have given up the *chiripá,* or green and blue skirt worn over the trouser seat like a flappy diaper. Factory-made clothes have relegated such heirlooms to rodeo parades and civic celebrations.

During rodeos, when skill in horsemanship bring prizes and fame to small-town workers, the *payador,* or broncobuster, becomes the star. He rides a wild horse into a tame trot, thrilling his Uruguayan audience in a manner similar to that of a star performer at a rodeo in the western states of North America.

Stock shows in Uruguay bring breeders from all over the republic and from neighboring Argentina to bid on prize animals. At the annual national livestock exposition in Montevideo, each August, a Hereford bull blue-ribbon winner can sell for up to $30,000, with Brazilian, Argentine, and U.S. breeders bidding against the wealthiest ranchers in Uruguay.

A typical Uruguayan ranch, or *estancia,* may include 65,000 acres, divided into two or three or four areas. Each area is supervised by a foreman, or *capataz,* the principal administrator under the ranch owners, or *estancieros,* who often are members of a family jointly owning and operating the ranch. Each *capataz* has the help of a few rangers, or *puesteros.* Each *puestero,* in turn, has charge of the hands tending the sheep or the cattle, or working the crops; for an Uruguayan *estancia* may have its largest sector given over to sheep, its next largest area for cattle grazing, and its smallest area for farm crops.

The *puestero* is the present-day successor of the old-time gaucho of literary and folk-song fame. Even now, the *puestero* spends his day in the saddle, checking the herds, supervising the vaccination of sheep and cattle, getting the hands to brand new livestock, and periodically checking to see that the fences are without gaps or getting them repaired if openings occur. Sometimes he drives a jeep, sometimes a truck, if not his horse. But he does not care to walk far.

WORKERS' BENEFITS

In 1943 the government began dependency allowances to the principal wage earner of families in the lowest economic brackets among urban workers. Not until 1954 were these same benefits extended to rural workers. Since then, farm and ranch workers can also receive a few pesos per month for each dependent child, dependent parent, or aged relative living in the same household, and for a wife expecting a child, if that family has an income considered at the poverty line by standards drawn up annually. Farm and ranch workers seasonally unemployed can also receive dependency allowances, in addition to unemployment-insurance payments.

Dependent children normally benefit from allowances only until they reach the age of fourteen, although they can help their underpaid fathers receive payments until their sixteenth birthday if they are enrolled in secondary school or a vocational training program. Here the inequities between urban and rural workers show up, for the children of low-paid or unemployed urban workers live near such schools, even in slum areas. Children of farm and ranch hands, by contrast, are much less likely to live near enough to postelementary schooling to ensure benefits to their low-income families from their fourteenth to their sixteenth birthdays.

Financial resources for the Dependency Allowance Funds come principally from taxes paid by employers on the salaries and wages of their employees. Again rural-urban inequities are frequent; for government and private companies in the cities, being part of the industrial tempo, more readily and more promptly pay such taxes. Ranch and farm owners often find a time lag between their getting their products to market and their receiving their payments, causing in turn a lag in their own tax payments. Rural Allowance Funds are consistently behind in collecting taxes from the ranch and farm owners and consistently late in making payments to low-paid hands and unemployed agricultural workers.

In the case of retired workers, urban pensioners also sometimes suffer a delay of one or two months in receiving their social security payments, but rural workers who retire suffer delays in receiving their pensions of several weeks beyond any waiting period found in the cities. With a national longevity of sixty-eight years, the problem of delayed pension payments to Uruguayans in their late fifties and early sixties has become a periodic administrative headache to the government agencies involved.

Plagued by hundreds of strikes each year, in recent years the Uruguayan economy has not been able to enjoy its potential earnings. Nor has the government been able to acquire sufficient tax revenues to pay for the elaborate system of welfare benefits. As a consequence, some ministries have not had enough funds on hand to meet their payrolls. Similarly, retirement funds have been so low that pensioners have had to wait two months or more to receive their checks.

Food price-support programs have helped the grocery retailers and middleman distributors more than they have the farm and ranch owners and workers. Subsidies also help keep the food bills of urban dwellers from rising beyond family incomes, but do not benefit as directly farm and ranch workers, who usually maintain truck gardens.

Some farm and ranch workers belong to the Wool Workers Federation or to the CONAPROLE Autonomous Workers Association, though these unions are run by the urban members and dominated by urban workers. With many ranches and farms organized so that each area of an *estancia* has a handful of workers under a foreman, the circumstances for large farm-ranch unions have not been promising. Through national legislation of administrations attuned to social welfare during most of this century, rural workers have been included in many of the programs enjoyed by urban workers, from social security to medical care. But, in terms of educational and hospital facilities, rural workers have never approached equality with their urban counterparts, who make up 80 percent of the working population.

Many farm and ranch workers are classified as "urban," for they often live in small towns near their work rather than on the *estancias* in isolated dwellings. Thus, numbers of agricultural workers are socially part of small-town life. And even unskilled rural workers by law are covered by minimum-wage standards, inhibiting somewhat the exploitation found in many other Latin American nations. Political commentators allude to the struggle between the capital and the *campo,* or countryside. But an accurate demographic assessment shows most Uruguayans living at least on the periphery of urban life.

BUSINESS LEADERSHIP

Like workers, business and industrial leaders have organized in order to make the collective voice of management heard. The National Chamber of Commerce speaks for retail merchants and wholesale distributors. Its affiliated chambers for each of the nineteen territorial departments are further subdivided into municipal Chambers of Commerce in each city, but the bulk of the membership is centered in Montevideo. Approximately 12 per cent of the total work force of the nation can be found in merchandising, but within these ranks clerks far outnumber managers or owners. Only management belongs to the Chamber of Commerce.

Foreign businessmen resident in Montevideo also maintain commercial associations, such as the U.S. Chamber of Commerce of Uruguay, which Morris Zimmelman has ably served as president for several years. This group has coordinated the efforts of Uruguayan and North American business leaders to promote cultural and commercial exchanges through the "Partners in the Alliance for Progress" program. Under this program, the state of Minnesota became the trade and cultural partner of Uruguay, with James Henry as executive director in Minneapolis and diplomat Domínguez Cámpora as head of the Uruguayan committee. Similar British, Italian, and Brazilian Chambers of Commerce promote trade between their respective countries and Uruguay.

Two effective business spokesmen are the *Liga de Defensa Comercial* (League of Commercial Defense) and the *Cámara Mercantil de los Productos del País* (Mercantile Chamber of Products of the Nation). The latter especially lobbies effectively with committees of the General Assembly and executive agencies on behalf of merchants. Its weekly information bulletin, *Semanario Informativo*, is rated one of the leading trade publications of Uruguay.

The *Cámara Nacional de Industrias* (National Chamber of Industries) speaks for the manufacturers of the nation, who employ 12 per cent of the full-time work force of Uruguay. Its executive committee meets each month to coordinate the stand on public issues affecting manufacturing that individual industries feel the chamber should take. The 1943 law that prompted the creation of the National Chamber of Industries stipulated that wage contracts would be established by tripartite Councils on Salaries, with representatives from labor unions, the government, and organized employer associations. Industries active in shaping chamber policy range from old-line textile manufacturers to the new automobile assembly plant in Colonia.

The National Chamber of Industries especially concerns itself with changes in export-import regulations and quotas. In April, 1959, the chamber led the fight that resulted in the abolition of the Export-Import Control Board. In July, 1967, the chamber consulted at length with the minister of industry and commerce and with the minister of finance before the Gestido administration decided on new import controls.

Away from Montevideo, one organization also speaks for provincial industrial and retail business interests combined, the Federation of Commercial and Industrial Entities of the Interior of the Country. The Association of Textile Industries of the Interior often acts in a semi-autonomous manner as a spokesman for provincial industrialists, yet it also coordinates its efforts as a component member of the National Chamber of Industries.

The Association of Banks includes both the government and private banks and speaks for all bank management in dealing with the politically powerful Union of Bank Employees. Government banks do 65 per cent of all commercial banking in Uruguay. Yet the number of private banks continues to grow. In September,

1960, there were fifty-eight private banks chartered in the republic. By September, 1967, that total had risen to sixty-four, most with several branches.

Dean of the private banks is the *Banco Comercial,* founded in 1857. Most modern in its operations perhaps is the First National City Bank of New York, whose Montevideo branch publishes a *Monthly Letter* whose statistics are sometimes more comprehensive than those of the government ministries. British, French, Italian, Dutch, and Argentine banks vie with Uruguayan private banks to make loans, attract savings and checking accounts, and underwrite mortgages. The annual yearbook published by the Association of Banks gives a picture of the over-all economic activity of the nation for the year.

Administrators of government banks have sometimes gone into the commercial field after several years of service. One of the longest tenures in government banking has been that of F. Simoens Arce, an accountant by profession, who served the Bank of the Republic for thirty years, from 1934 to 1964, much of that time as manager. Since 1964, he has been a top consultant to business and industry.

RANCH AND FARM GROUPS

Representing the landowners and ranchers, the *Asociación Rural,* founded in 1871, is oriented more to livestock and farming technology than to politics, although it does voice a position on some public issues before the legislature. With a reputation for defending rural traditions, the Rural Association maintains the nation's official registry for blooded and pedigreed livestock. Some of its members are leaders of Uruguayan upper-class society.

One example of a civic and social leader springing from the Rural Association is Hugo Romay Salvo, whose family-owned ranches in the department of Río Negro are among the most extensive in the nation. Romay Salvo himself owns and operates one of the commercial television stations of Montevideo, Channel 4, and its affiliate Radio Monte Carlo. The Salvo family has been perhaps the wealthiest in Uruguay, building the ornate Palacio

Salvo skyscraper in the heart of downtown Montevideo, topped with a TV antenna. Romay Salvo epitomizes those Uruguayan leaders who remain active in both ranching and commercial business, spending time both in the countryside and in the city, and working for organizations that speak for several interests.

Although three-fourths of all farms in Uruguay are less than 250 acres each, farm and ranch units of more than 12,500 acres each, though relatively few in number, take up 20 per cent of all agricultural land. A dozen leading aristocratic families still retain holdings of more than 100,000 acres each, such as the Damboriarena lands in the department of Rivera and the Martiricorena ranches and farms in the department of Artigas. But Uruguay is a nation whose population is overwhelmingly urban and middle class. Thus, the peon of other Latin American nations usually has risen, in Uruguay, to the status of *medianero,* or tenant farmer, and *puestero,* or assistant range foreman, just high enough up the occupational ladder to where he identifies somewhat with the foreman and not with day laborers.

Against this backdrop, two organizations have developed to speak for agricultural management and ownership in the political arena, the Rural Federation and the Federal League of Rural Action. The *Federación Rural,* politically conservative, has grown into the most politically active agrarian organization in Uruguay. It can be quite militant in debating public issues, yet suave in lobbying with legislative committees or the Ministry of Agriculture. The Federal League of Rural Action began to grow in 1951 as a lobby for ranchers. In 1954 it supported the Colorados, but by 1958 had crossed over to the Blancos. After 1964 it lost some of its political impact, but as late as 1968 was still lobbying.

THE FEMININE TOUCH

Among all Latin American nations, Uruguay, first gave women full political and economic equality with men. Able to vote, keep a bank account in her own name, or institute divorce proceedings for cruelty long before her counterparts in other Latin American nations could do so, the Uruguayan woman has had few public or private inequities to fight since the promulgation of the 1919 constitution. As a consequence, Uruguayan women have tended to assume some active leadership and extensive participation within the political parties, labor unions, business associations, and other organized interest groups open to the general public, rather than concentrate in women's political or vocational groups.

In the realm of charitable, civic, and social groups, women are especially numerous and often in charge. In the professions, Uruguayan women have long been active in medicine, law, dentistry, pharmacy, and government administration, but are more numerous in education, social work, and retail merchandising. As in most other countries, they almost monopolize nursing, home economics, and similar pursuits.

In public life, during the 1967–72 term of the national legislature, two women—Alba Roballo of the Colorado Unity Front and Elsa Fernández de Borges of the Colorado Unity and Reform—sit in the Senate. During the 1959–63 and 1963–67 terms, women also sat in the Senate, and for years have had representation in the Chamber of Deputies.

Senator Roballo's own career exemplifies the oportunities for women from families of low income to rise in public service to the nation. Her parents worked a small farm in the department of Artigas. Working her way through the College of Law in Montevideo, she became active in the Colorado Party. After serving as legal counsel in the Ministry of Finance, she rose to vice-chairman of the board of the Rural Retirement Fund, then to vice-chairman of the Departmental Council (plural executive) of Montevideo during 1954–58, and was elected to the Senate in 1962 and 1966. In 1968 she served in the cabinet of President Pacheco as minister of culture until her resignation in June in a protest over presidential curtailment of rioters.

MANY VOICES

If various interest groups in Uruguay seem to be talking all at once, the result is not cacophony. To those who listen, the noises are not harsh but meaningful. Uruguay does not achieve a consensus on controversies any easier than does any other democracy, for its representative government, tied to free speech and a free press, includes not only political moderates and traditional liberals and conservatives, but also smaller numbers of extremists. But anyone can make himself heard by at least some of his fellow Uruguayans.

Yet, because patronage still flourishes in the public sector and personal connections are as important in the private sector as they are anywhere else in the world, Uruguayans, like their counterparts in other nations, must organize to make their views felt in their land and must utilize their personal contacts to smooth their own paths to public or private influence. Opportunities to do so abound in a society not rigidly stratified.

VII

A Uruguayan Birthright: Education

In the Spanish colonial period and in the early years of the republic, Uruguay fared no better than most of the other Latin American nations in terms of formal educational facilities. Yet, by the 1960's, Uruguay led all other Latin American countries in adult literacy and in the proportion of its children in primary schools. Uruguay's emphasis on modern education began in the 1870's under the influence of schoolmaster José Pedro Varela, second only to statesman José Batlle as a maker of modern Uruguay.

The Jesuits had been Uruguay's first schoolteachers, and following their expulsion by the Spanish Government in 1773 for political reasons, Franciscans took over the schools. But formal schooling was for a small number of city boys who would serve the Church, the army, or the government. Most rural boys and the girls were not included.

As late as 1855, the handful of primary schools in Uruguay held less than seven pupils per 1,000 inhabitants. Until 1885, secondary education consisted of a few classrooms in which a small number of boys were prepared to pass the entrance examinations of universities. The University of the Republic itself was founded in Montevideo on July 18, 1849, the nineteenth university to be established in Latin America. The first faculty had two professors of medicine, two people teaching religion, and one teacher each for philosophy, mathematics, Latin, and political history. Not until the 1870's did Uruguayan leadership awake to the need for modern educational facilities.

José Varela was born in 1845 and lived only thirty-four years. But, when he died in 1879, he left a legacy for his country: the tradition that a public education is the political birthright of every citizen. After his own schooling in Montevideo, Varela in 1867 visited Europe, interviewing Victor Hugo about world literary trends. Then Varela visited the United States, where he met the distinguished Argentine statesman and educator, Domingo Faustino Sarmiento, then serving as Argentine minister to the United States. The twenty-three-year-old teacher became a disciple of the fifty-seven-year-old statesman, who himself helped make Argentina a literate and modern nation.

In 1868, Varela returned to Montevideo to begin his career as an educator. The Society of the Friends of Popular Education was formed with Varela as secretary, and in 1869 he became its president, establishing an experimental school to try out new teaching methods. Varela became the leader of Uruguayan educational thought in 1874, when his first book, *La Educación del Pueblo,* made the public aware of the nature of pedagogy. In 1876, Varela's second book, *Legislación Escolar,* proposed that the republic get a new school law. The next year, President Lorenzo Latorre carried out the suggestion by executive decree. In 1877 Varela was promoted to National Inspector of the Bureau of Primary Instruction, with authority to improve primary schools.

MORE CLASSROOMS, MORE TEACHERS

Working long hours every day of the week, with no vacations, Varela soon undermined his health. But, for two years, during 1877–79, he managed to interest scores of bright young Uruguayans in a teaching career through his periodical *Enciclopedia de Educación.* Classroom construction began to devour more government funds than the cautious politicians had budgeted. But

Varela's death in October, 1879, did not slow down the forces of reform that he had set in motion.

Teachers began to receive not only government assistance through a cabinet ministry, but also the backing of local groups similar to Parent-Teachers Associations in the United States. These Committees of Development, or *Fomento,* have linked neighborhood civic leadership to school administrators and teachers during the past ninety years.

In recent decades, the classical emphasis of routine memorization and rote recitation has been changed to extensive use of libraries and laboratories. Even after the era of Varela, for years the public educational system remained highly centralized in terms of control of textbooks, curriculums, and lesson plans. Identical examinations required for promotion to the next highest grade were given in all schools, in much the same manner as they were administered in France in the 1930's. But, since the 1950's, regional administrators have been able to adapt curriculums and testing to their own local circumstances.

For years the Ministry of Public Instruction headed the nation's school system, until the 1966 constitution created the Ministry of Culture. The new ministry is responsible for public instruction, as well as for libraries, museums, and fine-arts facilities. It coordinates four councils for primary, secondary, vocational, and higher education, to ensure decentralized control over public education.

PRIMARY EDUCATION

The National Council of Primary and Normal Instruction (*Consejo Nacional de Enseñanza Primaria y Normal*) has a director general and four other members, plus a professional staff. The council directs a Corps of Inspectors, with each territorial department of the republic having a regional director. The corps is organized by subject matter so that an inspector of mathematics supervises teachers in that subject in all six primary grades of a municipality.

Although Uruguay has achieved an adult literacy rate of 92

per cent and has almost 90 per cent of its children ages six through eight in primary schools, classrooms are crowded. The result has been double or triple sessions in some schools, with some students arriving in the early morning, then giving up the classroom to a second group for the afternoon, and then having the same classroom house a third group in the evening.

In 1949, there were 122 children for each public primary classroom in use in the republic. By 1967, the ratio had been lowered to 102. The improvement was achieved by the Ministry of Public Works' speeding up construction of schools in the departments of Mercedes, Colonia, and Artigas, where the greatest shortage of classrooms had existed. The shortage was also relieved by the purchase of large residences, which have been converted into classroom buildings.

In 1947, the dropout rate after the third grade was still steep, with only one-fourth of the students who entered the first grade later graduating from the sixth grade. By 1959, the situation had improved enough in Montevideo so that half of the entering firstgraders were graduated from the sixth grade. By 1967, the Montevideo dropout rate had been reduced still further. Away from Montevideo, the provincial city and rural ratios were not as good. Rural primary schools often contain only five grades, with graduates then going directly to vocational schools.

The National Primary Education Council also administers the normal schools, which train teachers for primary schools and kindergartens. In Montevideo and a few other cities, public kindergartens are maintained for children ages three through five. In the departments where appropriations cannot finance instruction adequately, plans for kindergartens have been suspended.

In Salto, for example, in 1960 departmental inspectors had recommended the establishment of kindergartens, but the regular primary-school appropriations were so slim that the number of free notebooks issued had to be cut to two per student. Even the customary free pencils had not been distributed in the Salto primary schools, causing the cancelation of any kindergarten plans.

Free lunches are provided for primary-school children unable to purchase their own; and, for students with lunch money, the cost of a meal at a school cafeteria is kept to a minimum through government subsidies. A Children's Council *(Consejo del Niño)* establishes the dietary requirements for pupils to bolster good health.

To minimize the discomfort that poor students might feel in the presence of wealthier children whose clothes are of higher quality, primary-school administrators encourage the use of school smocks, which, as civilian-type uniforms worn over regular clothing, engender a school spirit and seem to boost the morale of those not well dressed.

SECONDARY EDUCATION

The National Council of Secondary Education *(Consejo Nacional de Enseñanza Secundaria)* is headed by a director general and six members. Three of these council members are elected by the secondary-school teachers of the nation, and the other three by the other three national councils of primary, vocational, and university education.

Secondary education in Uruguay is organized into a two-step pattern: a *liceo* of four years and a preparatory school of two years. A student completing the six-year sequence is awarded a *bachillerato*, or academic diploma approaching in liberal-arts orientation two years of undergraduate college in the United States but officially recognized as the equivalent of a high school education.

The *liceo* is patterned somewhat after a French *lycée*, with some British influence and some U.S. high school and junior college ideas evidenced. As with the primary schools, Uruguayan secondary schools are more book-centered than their U.S. counterparts, with strenuous homework and a minimum of extracurricular activities encroaching on academic time. *Preparatorio* is preuniversity training designed to give the student a liberal-arts education so that during his university years he can concentrate on professional subjects.

From 1849 to 1877, the University of the Republic directly controlled all secondary education. From the era of Varela to 1935, the secondary and university educational administrations were separate but closely connected. In 1935, the National Council of Secondary Education received its present autonomy, as did the university.

No professional pedagogical training was provided for secondary-school teachers until 1949, when the Artigas Institute of Professors (*Instituto de Profesores Artigas*) was established. Secondary-school faculty members were often part-time and were paid on the basis of the number of courses taught and the number of hours spent in contact with students. Since the advent of the institute, the number of full-time secondary-school teachers has increased manyfold. All prospective secondary-school teachers must hold a university degree and must take a competitive examination in their subject areas, with those with the highest marks being given preference for job openings.

VOCATIONAL EDUCATION

Only unofficially is the third council known as the Vocational Education Council. Officially it is the National Council of the Labor University (*Consejo Nacional de la Universidad del Trabajo*), established in 1942. Some of the vocational schools affiliated with the Labor University themselves date back to 1856 and 1877. In the 1890's, these trade schools, originally created to rehabilitate teenage boys considered to be delinquents, were changed to institutions striving to provide industrial and agricultural trade skills to youth not able to prepare for the professional courses of the university.

The average age of students entering secondary schools of the *liceo-preparatorio* sequence is twelve, and the average age of entering university freshmen is eighteen. At age eleven, students with five years of primary school can enter a Labor University vocational school for up to six years of training.

The *Universidad del Trabajo del Uruguay* (UTU) administers six large vocational schools in Montevideo and forty-two others in provincial towns, with course offerings somewhat resembling those in the vocational high schools of the United States. Curriculums include public-health nursing and hospital administration, carpentry, automobile and heavy-machinery mechanics, electricity, and radio repair. In the semirural areas, UTU also administers twenty-three agricultural schools, which teach animal husbandry, soil conservation, and milk production.

In June, 1967, Professor Luis Víctor Anastasia became director general, or executive head, of the Labor University and within one month had initiated more proposals for curricular modernization than had been evidenced for a decade previous. The National Council of the Labor University promptly approved the changes advocated by the thirty-six-year-old dynamic educator. As a consequence, the vocational schools now offer training in shipbuilding techniques. A shortage of trained metal workers who could handle ship repairs had prompted the hiring of Argentine and Brazilian technicians temporarily at the Montevideo repair docks. Now Uruguay produces enough ship repairmen of its own.

Since 1967 the agricultural schools of the UTU also have modernized their offerings to include new courses in poultry science. Uruguay has long depended on its sheep and cattle as livestock mainstays. Now, chicken and turkey production has been increased to aid the domestic consumers markets.

UNIVERSITY EDUCATION

Higher education in Uruguay centers in the University of the Republic, in Montevideo. The Central University Council (*Consejo Central Universitario*), its governing body, is the fourth coordinate council working with the Ministry of Culture, from a position of autonomy. The only recognized degree-granting university in the nation, the University of the Republic was formally inaugurated in 1849, but the first university training in Uruguay began in 1838 in the fields of medicine, philosophy, mathematics, and political economy.

Under its 1849 organization as a full-fledged university, the first professional school to be founded was that of law, with medicine being added as a component college in 1875. By 1908 a new law gave autonomy in academic matters to each college of the university. The rector of the university, however, would be appointed by the president of the republic, with confirmation by the Senate of the national legislature. With new-found freedom to innovate on the part of college deans, the university then began to expand to its current ten colleges.

Under the 1908 reform, alumni could be elected to the Central University Council for the first time. And student representatives were elected to the Advisory Council, or *Claustro,* of each college. The first student admitted as a member of an Advisory Council with a vote equal to that of faculty representatives joined the *Claustro* of the College of Dentistry in 1921. In 1958 the present Organic Law of the University came into effect, giving student representatives full membership in the Central University Council, as well as in the General Assembly of the college *Claustros.*

As in many other Latin American nations, Uruguayan university students have come to believe that they have a right to participate in the policy-making of the university. Consequently, street demonstrations concerning both academic matters and political questions of a national and international scope have recurred several times a year in recent years. Since the 1958 reform giving students an official voice in the Central University Council, student demonstrations have increased, though prior to the enactment of the 1958 law its advocates contended that bringing student representatives into the bodies making policy would diminish the circumstances causing their frustration.

In March, 1960, the state visit of U.S. President Eisenhower prompted university students to suspend classes, to pressure the national government to show their displeasure over U.S. policies in Latin America. Older citizens who defended the student protest claimed that the illiberal image of the Eisenhower regime had provoked the students. Yet in June, 1961, groups of students took similar action when a widely admired liberal statesman, Adlai Stevenson, paid a visit to Montevideo.

On July 26, 1967, student groups divided sharply over Fidel

Castro's Communist government in Cuba. To some students, Castro still loomed as a folk hero from a small nation able to defy the large and powerful United States. A majority of the students, however, opposed Castro but did not challenge well-organized small groups who put up Castroite banners inside university buildings. At the College of Law and Social Sciences, the banners and posters were hung, but at the College of Economic Sciences and Administration not one poster was displayed. Architecture students ignored the controversy entirely.

From time to time, conservative critics have charged the existence of strong Communist influence both within the faculty and within the Federation of University Students, although specific names and examples seldom are cited in letters to the editor, columns, or newspaper editorials. Communist Party members are active in student organizations beyond any doubt, though their number has remained small.

As an engineer attuned more to scientific and industrial issues than to social ones, University President Oscar Maggiolo has tried to dispel the impression that the university has come under Communist influence. His predecessor as rector, Mario A. Cassinoni, active in the Socialist Party, attempted to refute similar accusations in a 1959 booklet *Ordenanza de elecciones universitarias.*

During the last week of October, 1967, University President Maggiolo demonstrated that he would not remain silent in the name of academic freedom as had Cassinoni on some occasions. Fifty students held a wake for Ernesto "Ché" Guevara, Communist guerrilla leader whose death had been announced in Bolivia. Maggiolo called the interruption of classes an "abuse of academic freedom" and tendered his resignation as president of the university as his own protest. Larger numbers of students and faculty begged him to remain at his post, which Maggiolo consented to do, strengthening the anti-Communist elements at the university. In November, 1968, the university's Central Council gave Maggiolo a vote of confidence.

Political postures of the faculty within each college vary from right wing to left wing, with a majority of the professors generally considered to be liberals or moderates within the Uruguayan political spectrum. No political polarization by college has evidenced itself, but the more left-wing students and faculty have tended to come from the College of Law and Social Sciences, whereas the more conservative elements have tended to come from the College of Economic Sciences and Administration, with its attunement to business and industry.

Often considered the leader of university liberal sentiment in the 1960's is Saúl D. Cestau, dean of the College of Law and Social Sciences. Typifying the moderates whose expertise propels them into government advisory posts is Enrique Grunhut, professor of chemistry with postdoctoral work at the University of Notre Dame in the United States. Grunhut, as a member of the National Atomic Energy Commission, has brought the university's physical-science research programs into rapport with government and industry.

Ernesto Onetto Rodríguez, dean of the College of Chemistry (which includes the School of Pharmacy), emphasizes industrial chemistry. Leopoldo C. Artucio, dean of the School of Architecture, stresses modern, functional designs found in newer apartment and office buildings and low-rent government housing units.

Hermógenes Alvarez, dean of the College of Medicine, has brought more clinical laboratory time to his senior students than can be found in the medical schools in other Latin American republics, his standards approximating some of the professional rigors of U.S. and Western European medical schools. As a consequence, graduates of the University of the Republic pursuing postgraduate medical studies abroad have enjoyed the reputation of being the best prepared young physicians coming from Latin America. The College of Medicine maintains the gigantic *Hospital de Clínicas* in Batlle Park as both a center for research and as a low-cost medical-service center for working-class patients. Twenty-two stories high, with 3,100 beds, this hospital, completed in

1950, was designed as one of the most modern medical facilities in Latin America.

José Postiglioni, dean of the College of Veterinary Medicine, works closely with the government's Ministry of Livestock-raising and Agriculture in advancing the techniques of animal husbandry. Rodolfo V. Tálice, dean of the College of Humanities and Sciences, in the 1960's has encouraged the growth of special institutes to relate graduate research to national problems. For example, under the direction of Professor Eugenio Petit Muñoz, the Institute of Historical Research has made available archival materials through paperback reprints. Springing from the College of Economic Sciences and Administration, an Institute of Economic Investigation has been directed by Enrique Iglesias, head of the nation's Central Bank.

Director of the Vázquez Acevedo Institute, the preparatory school operated by the university to set the academic pace for other preparatories, is Hugo Fernández Artucio. For twenty-five years prior to his resignation in June, 1966, Fernández had been an editor of the republic's leading daily newspaper, *El Día*. As an educational administrator, he typifies the Uruguayan tendency to staff its institutions of learning with "men of public affairs," civic leaders who bridge the gap between academic and public life with the skill of a renaissance man.

The president of the university is by law also head of the Central University Council, which is composed of two delegates from each of the colleges, one of which must be the dean of each college. The ten colleges of the university, in the chronological order of their founding, are: Law and Social Sciences, 1849; Medicine, 1875; Engineering, 1915; Architecture, 1915; Agriculture, 1925; Chemistry and Pharmacy, 1929; Dentistry, 1929; Economic Sciences and Administration, 1932; Veterinary Medicine, 1933; and Humanities and Sciences, 1945.

No unified campus exists. The principal buildings serving as university headquarters house the College of Economic Sciences and Administration and the College of Law and Social Sciences, the president of the university and his administrative staff, some of the faculties of humanities and sciences, and branch libraries of law, economics, and humanities. These buildings face onto the main street of Montevideo, 18 de Julio, adjacent to the National Library. In other parts of the city are separate facilities for the professional schools. The dentistry, agriculture, and architecture facilities are each miles apart.

In July, 1967, University President Maggiolo disclosed the detailed plan for restructuring the university so that in the 1970's a central campus will allow more efficient use of equipment and resources by related academic disciplines. A central library, supplemented by more-specialized collections for each professional school, will better utilize the documentation now fragmented into small libraries. Limited funds for book acquisitions must be dissipated somewhat, as general references are now duplicated in each of the small professional libraries. In curricular matters, the *Plan de Reestructuración de la Universidad* would provide more opportunities for postgraduate research for those awarded professional degrees, including the offering of a doctorate in many fields not now represented.

Most university courses of study are geared to the professions and run six years, at the completion of which a student must defend his thesis in some facet of his profession. Thereupon, he is awarded a degree as Doctor of Medicine, Doctor of Dentistry, Licentiate in Law, Economist, Architect, Mathematician, Chemist and Pharmacist, Biologist, Civil Engineer, and so on.

EDUCATIONAL CRISIS: TEACHERS' SALARIES

From the mid-1950's into the late 1960's, the public-school teachers of Uruguay, like all other salaried employees in the republic, have received pay raises from time to time, to help teachers try to keep up with the continuing inflation. But the educators' unions have not been as successful as the trade unions of utility and industrial workers in bridging the economic gap and, as a consequence, many teachers have found their purchasing power eroding faster than that of day laborers. Compounding the crisis have been periods in which teachers had to wait weeks for back salary when public funds became depleted.

The national economy of Uruguay began to feel the impact of inflation around 1957, and by 1960 teachers were complaining that in terms of purchasing power they were no longer middle class but lower class. On August 28, 1963, for the first time in the history of Uruguay, teachers and administrators, in staging a walkout, actually closed down the school system of the nation for forty-eight hours. In walkouts and strikes both before and since, some schools have temporarily closed their doors; but no other work stoppage by educators has ever equaled that first action, when every secondary school in the republic shut down, as did 95 per cent of all elementary schools.

The cost of living had risen 12.7 per cent during the first half of 1963, and the public-school teachers had failed to receive a pay raise to offset this inflation. Intensifying teacher frustration was government insistence that 13 per cent of the teachers' salaries must be deducted during 1963 for the retirement fund, after earlier announcements by the administration had indicated that such deductions might be delayed because of the inflation.

After two days, the big shutdown of the schools ended, and the teachers had a pay raise. By spring, 1964, the teachers were again protesting their economic plight. The *Asociación Integremial de Enseñanza Secundaria,* the secondary-school teachers' union, announced in early April, 1964, that its members would strike at regular intervals if their paychecks were not received by the tenth of each month as their contract stipulated. That month paychecks were two weeks late and the secondary-school teachers went on strike for several days. Again in July, 1964, paychecks were late, and again secondary-school teachers went on strike for seventy-two hours. (In Uruguay the school year runs from February to December, with the summer months of December and January being vacation time.)

From 1965 through 1968, other teacher strikes occurred, most of them by the secondary-school teachers either to protest late payments of salaries or to demand higher pay raises to compensate for the growing inflation that continued to erode their purchasing power.

ADULT EDUCATION

Despite some financial difficulties, public vocational schools and some regular secondary schools have continued their programs of adult education in nighttime courses. Whatever a Uruguayan may lack in financial solvency, he never feels impoverished culturally or educationally.

In 1967, almost 3,900 students aged nine to seventy-five were learning English at one of the four buildings in Montevideo of the *Alianza Cultural Uruguay–Estados Unidos,* the Uruguayan–United States Cultural Alliance, a binational center supported by both the U.S. Government and private Uruguayan citizens. Since its inauguration in September, 1939, this center has drawn thousands of Uruguayans to its headquarters at number 1281 Paraguay Street in downtown Montevideo and to its twenty-six provincial affiliates in the interior of Uruguay. In addition, each Saturday the center reaches thousands of others with its broadcasts over Radio Carve, with an intensive English conversation course. These successful programs are also recorded and distributed on tapes and records.

In a similar manner, the Anglo-Uruguayan Cultural Institute, jointly financed by the British Government and private Uruguayan citizens, offers courses in English language and literature at its center in Montevideo and at its branch centers in Salto and Paysandú. Similarly, the French, Italian, and Brazilian governments jointly finance adult-education programs in cooperation with associations of Uruguayan civic leaders.

The Uruguay-Soviet Institute ostensibly has been set up to foster understanding of the Russian language and culture, but its emphasis has been on Communist political propaganda, with some fine-arts exhibits in recent years. The School of Social Work, maintained by the Ministry of Culture, also includes short courses for nonprofessional adults who wish to volunteer their services in slum areas for work with the aged or delinquent teenagers.

Mrs. A. Mazzella de Bevilacqua, director of the *Instituto Normal Superior,* the Advanced Education Institute for teacher training, in mid-1967 expanded the school's activities to include more short courses for adults seeking self-improvement in evening classes, as well as more special lectures for teachers wishing in-service updating on educational psychology.

Uruguayan Schools of Nursing, set up for regular full-time students aiming to be registered nurses, also maintain extra classes in practical nursing for adults interested in that field. Various series of lectures and demonstrations designed for adult education appear regularly on Channel 5, SODRE-TV, the government-owned and -operated television station. SODRE, the government-owned and -operated broadcasting entity, in its own auditoriums and conference halls, promotes music-appreciation adult education. Through its division for fine arts and for museums and libraries, the Ministry of Culture maintains an active program of adult education, ranging from art lessons to music appreciation.

One clue to the importance of formal education in the Uruguayan way of life can be found in the national government's annual budgets. In 1951, 19 per cent of the total expenditures went into the fields of education. In the 1967 national budget, that proportion had risen to 26.9 per cent of the total budget of the government.

Libraries

At the apex of the Uruguayan public-library system is the National Library, professionally directed for many years by Dionisio Trillo Pays, who in 1967 was still supplementing official funds with skillfully induced contributions from philanthropists to acquire a balanced cross section of modern technological and classical literature in the library's holdings, which number more than 300,000 volumes, plus a large archive of historical documentation. The Legislative Library, maintained at the capital primarily for the use of members of the General Assembly and the cabinet ministries, has almost 200,000 volumes.

The department of Montevideo government maintains branch public libraries in every sector of the capital city. And, unlike many other Latin American nations, where books must be used on the premises, Uruguay's public libraries put into practice the circulation of books. A small fee for a library card, with data on file identifying the borrower as a responsible citizen, entitles users of the major libraries to check out books for home reading.

Opened in 1943, the Artigas-Washington Library is maintained by the U.S. Information Service for use by the general public. Its holdings of more than 25,000 books circulate among 200,000 Uruguayans annually. The Artigas-Washington Library also operates a phonograph-record library and further promotes musical appreciation through concerts in its own auditorium. Most of the library's books are in English, but graduates of the American and British schools of Montevideo are joined by thousands of graduates of Uruguayan public and private schools, which require a reading knowledge of English for graduation.

A cultural and educational landmark rises from an old gray building in the heart of Montevideo, in the Plaza Libertad, not far from Kilometer Zero, from which all land distances are measured in Uruguay. Symbolically, the *Ateneo,* or Anthenaeum, founded in 1880, has been central in the intellectual life of the nation, fostering conferences, lectures, recitals, and short courses, all free to the general public.

The Ministry of Culture in 1943 created the National Academy of Letters to promote the literary culture of the nation. In 1945, the creation of a Commission of Literary Investigations further increased the desire of many adults to write or to receive some instruction in the appreciation of the literature of the Western world. Both the academy and the commission helped the growth of special libraries of contemporary novelists, playwrights, and essayists. Headquartered in Montevideo, the International American Institute for the Protection of Children maintains a specialized library on child care of 20,000 volumes, being one of the best such collections in the world.

Despite the strikes in recent years of teachers beset by inflation and delayed salary payments, and despite some attrition in numbers from the primary to the secondary schools, Uruguay among all Latin American nations has achieved universal adult literacy and the national birthright of some formal education for almost every child.

VIII

Cultural Expression:
From Literature to Television

Uruguay contained no great Indian civilizations that in Peru
and Mexico mixed with Spanish culture to produce painting,
music, and architecture vivid with the hybrid qualities of native
and Hispanic overtones. But, as a literate nation, Uruguay grew
from learning to literature. And, like its population, Uruguay's
cultural expression stems from European origins.

As in Argentina, so in Uruguay, colorful gauchos riding the
range inspired some folk music. But Uruguayan aspirations have
made their impact on people within the republic, elsewhere in
Latin America, and to some extent in Europe and the United
States not through music or other fine arts, but through the skill-
ful pens of Uruguayan writers.

Uruguay's cultural expression, which has flourished most in its
literature, has not been the property of a tiny elite, isolated
politically and personally from the rank-and-file citizenry of the
nation. In this republic, cultural expression has been broadly
based in terms of support, participation, and appreciation.

The European influences in writing and speech patterns especially accent Italian words. As in Buenos Aires, so too in Montevideo, the usual farewell is *chao,* from the Italian *ciao.* Even the
traditional Hispanic farewell of *adiós* has become *addio.* But in

hundreds of subtle ways, ranging from gestures to facial expressions, the people of the Banda Oriental have taken Spanish, Italian, and other European literary and cultural endeavors and given them a Uruguayan stamp.

JOSÉ ENRIQUE RODÓ

The giant of Uruguayan literature and one of the most distinguished men of letters in all of Latin America, José Enrique Rodó, who lived from 1872 to 1917, was the first great literary apostle of New Worldism or Latin Americanism. On the fiftieth anniversary of his death—May 1, 1967—Rodó still cast a giant philosophical shadow over the intellectuals of Uruguay and of most other Latin American nations, as evidenced by the outpouring of tributes. A half-century after his passing and more than two-thirds of a century after the publication of his best-known essay, José Rodó remains a literary figure of the first magnitude.

An artist with words, Rodó's fame originated in a 141-page book published in 1900, *Ariel,* an essay praising the use of leisure time for the pursuit of spiritual and intellectual contemplation. Rodó characterized the United States as materialistic, a mundane Caliban to be contrasted unfavorably with the idealistic Ariel— the prototype of Latin America. His characters were from Shakespeare's *The Tempest.*

A few decades before, Argentine educator Sarmiento and his Uruguayan disciple Varela had advocated that Latin America should take the United States as its model for national development, based on the gigantic technological strides that had brought the average North American a higher standard of living than his South American counterpart enjoyed. Then, at the turn of this century, the emergence of the United States as a world power had been dramatized through the Spanish-American War and the presence of U.S. troops in Puerto Rico and Cuba.

At this juncture in history, Rodó captured the attention of the Hispanic world with his essay stressing the inadequacy of mere technical progress yielding wealth and power. The Uruguayan wordsmith reaffirmed the value of the humanist in society, and thereby furnished balm to feelings of defensiveness by calling on Latin Americans to create their own "aristocracy of the spirit." *Ariel* became widely read from Mexico to Chile for decades and, even as late as the 1940's and 1950's, loomed as the ethical Bible of Latin American intellectuals.

At the turn of the century, the brashness of Theodore Roosevelt's Big Stick foreign policy in Latin America understandably engendered apprehension in Rodó. In the 1960's, when Fidel Castro's meetings in Havana openly call for guerrilla warfare against established regimes of the hemisphere — including the moderately liberal reform governments in Venezuela, Colombia, and Chile — perhaps Rodó will be read in a new light. After all, he wrote of the cultural influence of a larger and more prosperous nation upon its smaller neighbors. And he did remind his readers that the United States had nurtured religious liberty, education for all citizens, and the dignity of honest labor.

By the time his *El Mirador de Próspero* appeared in 1913, Rodó had become the acknowledged master in the use of prose in the Spanish-speaking world. Nicaraguan poet Rubén Darío called Rodó "the Latin American Emerson." Other leading men of letters compared Rodó to Carlyle and Macauley.

Although much of his time was spent writing or reading, Rodó did manage to lead a successful teaching and political career, a fact easily overshadowed by his literary fame. He became Professor of Literature at the University of the Republic in 1898, took over the post of director of the National Library in 1900, and served as a deputy in the legislature of the republic during 1902–5 and 1908–11. And during 1909 Rodó headed the *Círculo de la Prensa,* the Press Association.

The era of Rodó was the golden age of Uruguayan literature. Among his contemporaries was Julio Herrera y Reissig (1875–1910), who led a group of Bohemian poets who influenced poetry everywhere in Latin America. Among the novelists and short-story writers, Horacio Quiroga (1878–1937) brilliantly dealt with local rural life. An entire generation of Uruguayan writers stressed the colloquial culture of their region, romanticizing the Uruguayan countryside in the minds of millions of Latin Americans from the Rio Grande to Tierra del Fuego.

FLORENCIO SÁNCHEZ

Another contemporary of Rodó was Florencio Sánchez, who lived from 1875 to 1910. A playwright, Sánchez became the best-known dramatist of South America through his rough-and-ready plays, whose action is set in the Río de la Plata region. His Uruguayan, Argentine, and Paraguayan characters were realistic, yet contained a universal appeal among working men in many other countries. Professional and university theaters from Mexico City to Buenos Aires for decades kept Florencio Sánchez plays in production.

Through lively dialogue and the poignancy of social problems of average low-income families, Sánchez put the slums of Buenos Aires or Montevideo into a perspective that still seems timely in the light of urbanization in the 1960's. His *En Familia* and *Los Derechos de la Salud,* like many of his other plays, reflect city life. His *La Gringa, Barranca Abajo,* and *M'Hijo el Dotor* have a rural setting and portray the conflict between traditional creole ways of life and the innovations brought from the city. Sixty years later, social scientists were writing of the passing of traditional societies under the impact of modern standards, though less eloquently than Florencio Sánchez had been able to phrase the conflict.

In his *Los Muertos,* a drama of the moral disintegration of an alcoholic, Sánchez again anticipated by two-thirds of a century a social problem that commands the attention of the writers of our own time. The hero of *Los Muertos,* Lisandro, lacks the will power to stop drinking excessively, for through liquor he escapes his many problems for the moment. Sánchez unfolded his dialogue so that alcoholism itself does not become the sole target of the condemnation of a rigid moralist speaking early in this century.

Rather, alcoholism is treated with pity, as the circumstantial doom that awaits those who cannot learn to face the problems of modern society pressing around them.

Drama critics from distinguished newspapers of Latin America and Europe — *La Prensa* of Buenos Aires, *El Mercurio* of Santiago, *Le Monde* of Paris, and *Corriere della Sera* of Milan — have compared Florencio Sánchez to Dante, Dostoevsky, and Gorky for his skill in portraying an average man caught in a swirl of circumstances from which he cannot pry himself loose. In *Nuestros Hijos,* a play about illegitimate children, Sánchez anticipated modern social workers in considering these offspring as the victims of their environment.

Juan Zorrilla de San Martín

An outstanding writer from the latter part of the nineteenth century, Juan Zorrilla de San Martín remained prominent in this century partly because of his career as a diplomat. He lived from 1855 to 1931. A romantic poet known throughout Latin America, Zorrilla de San Martín first captured fame through his patriotic ode *La Leyenda Patria,* written in 1879. On many occasions, those in charge of various civic ceremonies in Montevideo had Zorrilla recite this work.

In 1888, Zorrilla wrote a long poetic legend, *Tabaré,* based on a theme of the Charrúas, the Indians of Uruguay at the time that the Spaniards arrived. At first only in Paraguay, where Guaraní Indian culture was similar to the Charrúa, did the Zorrilla composition become a classic. But then the *littérateur* leadership of Argentina discovered *Tabaré* and spread its lyrical beauty from Chile to Colombia through Buenos Aires periodicals.

Zorrilla, after a secondary-school education in Montevideo, received his university education in Chile, and reflected a broad South American phraseology, rather than the regional Plata one, in his writings. In 1878, he founded the Montevideo daily newspaper *El Bien Público.* In the 1900's and 1920's, Zorrilla served with distinction as a diplomat, being the Uruguayan ambassador to the Vatican, to France, and to Spain, as well as its spokesman in numerous international gatherings from the League of Nations to treaty conferences.

His son, José Luis Zorrilla de San Martín, carried on the creativity of the family though not as a writer; he created one of the landmark pieces of sculpture of Montevideo, the statue of the gaucho on horseback at the intersection of 18 de Julio and Constituyente avenues. Another Zorrilla de San Martín, Alejandro, has enjoyed a distinguished career in government, serving as a deputy in the lower chamber of the legislature from 1955 to 1963, as foreign minister of Uruguay during 1963-65, and as a senator from the Blanco Party during the 1967–72 term. Still another Zorrilla de San Martín, China, has become the leading stage and television actress of Uruguay.

Modern Novelists

Perhaps the greatest of Uruguay's modern novelists was Eduardo Acevedo Díaz, who lived from 1851 to 1924. A diplomat, politician, and soldier, Acevedo Díaz is remembered best as the author of the novel about the life of the gauchos, *Soledad,* written in 1894. With cattle and sheep ranges as a setting, the gaucho characters brought into focus the rugged provincial life of yesteryear that stretched across the pampa of Uruguay and Argentina. Acevedo Díaz also wrote a historical trilogy, which he called a "hymn of blood," covering the epoch of the Uruguayan struggle for independence against the greater power of Spain, Argentina, and then Brazil. These three novels were *Ismael, Nativa,* and *Grito de Gloria.*

Another novelist, Javier de Viana, who lived from 1872 to 1925, captured the spirit of the gaucho at a later period of Uruguayan history, as the modern civilization of the late nineteenth century evaporated the romantic, rural life on the range. Viana's *Gaucha* has been one of the few South American novels compared to the works of Emile Zola by numerous critics, who see in it the same kind of skilled characterization of downtrodden heroes and heroines found in the works of the famed French novelist. Viana also won fame for his short stories, especially a volume called *Leña Seca.*

Another Uruguayan novelist, Carlos Reyles, who lived from 1868 to 1938, won fame not only in Latin America and Spain but also to a modest degree in the United States, Canada, and Britain when his novel *El Embrujo de Sevilla* (*The Witchery of Seville*) was translated into English and published under the title *Castanets.* Reyles' novel *Beba* gained him fame as the writer of a psychological commentary on the problems of family inbreeding. Reyles, in his novel *El gaucho florido,* captured in vivid detail the picture of the countryside over which the Uruguayan cowboy roamed, a vast plain of lonely grassland, with more sheep and cattle than humans for company.

CARLOS VAZ FERREIRA

Carlos Vaz Ferreira, who lived from 1873 to 1959, is one of the leading philosophers produced in Latin America since the early nineteenth century. As W. Rex Crawford put it, like Rodó, Vaz Ferreira had extreme sensitivity to periods of crisis, and emphasized the fluid, living, and "never-completed character of thought," a hesitancy to draw general conclusions, which springs from depth, not from superficiality.*

A distinguished professor at the University of the Republic, Vaz Ferreira taught philosophy at the time when positivism engulfed the thinking of intellectuals in South America. In the 1890's, these positivists embraced a philosophy dedicated to verifiable experience, repudiating revealed religion as the basis for human insight. After reading the books of French philosopher Auguste Comte, positivists emphasized a faith in humanism and material progress.

After dozens of Uruguayan intellectuals had studied in Vaz Ferreira's philosophy course, the university in 1913 decided to make his stimulating mind available to a wider audience and creat-

* See W. Rex Crawford, *A Century of Latin American Thought* (rev. ed.; New York: Frederick A. Praeger, 1966), pp. 90–94.

ed the *Catédra de Maestro de Conferencias,* or Professorship of Master of Conferences, so that he could be paid a regular salary while being free to preside over various meetings of nonstudents as well as students and faculty. This action was a Uruguayan forerunner of more recently endowed professorships in the United States that go beyond traditional departments and colleges so that an outstanding scholar might enrich research efforts from various related fields.

Vaz Ferreira began as a disciple of John Stuart Mill and moved to a flexible position accepting positivism but not any dogmatic determinism. With the publication of English and French translations of his 1909 book, *Lógica viva* (Living Logic) , he captured a North American and European following. The second edition of *Lógica viva,* published in 1920, provoked debates at Oxford, and focused the attention of Mexican, Chilean, and Argentine scholars on the university in Montevideo. Colombians and Italians began to quote his concept of "the illusion of experience," the belief that to base living on a dogma strengthens belief in it, just as if that dogma had been proved experimentally. Vaz Ferreira had bridged the gap between the positivists of the 1890's and the modern philosophers of the 1920's. In his 1940 edition of *Fermentario (Mind Vat)* , he observed that people speak of men of thought and men of action as distinctly opposed to each other, but "men of thought are also men of action, the action working a different way."

From 1929 to 1941, he was president of the university from time to time, and, from 1945 to his death in 1959, he was dean of the College of Humanities. Inspired by Vaz Ferreira, South Americans began to feel that some theoretical men might be the most "practical" men after all, for their actions were so long-ranged as to be misunderstood by their "practical" critics, who demanded quick solutions to life's complicated problems.

JOSÉ PEDRO MASSERA

José Pedro Massera, who lived from 1866 to 1942, is not as well known outside Uruguay as are his countrymen Rodó and Vaz

Ferreira, but within his native land Massera loomed large as a philosopher and writer. From 1887 to 1927 he taught philosophy at the University of the Republic. Although Massera gave up teaching in 1927 to pursue his political career in the Senate, he never stopped writing essays and books, which stimulated some of the civic and academic leaders of Uruguay.

Massera began as a devotee of positivism and became an idealist calling for a coexistence of science and humanism in which human relationships must try to catch up with scientific advancements. In a general way, he anticipated the writings along this line in the 1950's and 1960's by the British writer C. P. Snow.

In 1920, Massera's *Reflexiones sobre Rodó* helped a newer generation understand the deeper meaning of the philosophy of Rodó. The generation of the 1920's groped for a political philosophy to bring the inter-American system headed by the Pan American Union into a focus reflecting the ideals of the League of Nations. After World War I, the various nations of the Western Hemisphere pondered peaceful means for settling disputes not only among themselves but among nations of the world. They went back to Rodó through Massera's book.

In many essays on the pedagogy of Uruguay, Massera forced educators to realize the lack of scientific methodology evidenced in much of the nation's higher education. He engendered a clamor for laboratory sciences. In recent decades, medical education in Uruguay, for example, has been rated among the best in Latin America because of the clinical laboratory emphasis, contrasting with too few clinic hours and too many lecture hours in most other Latin American nations.

RECENT WRITERS

Alberto Zum Felde, an outstanding literary critic and social historian, born in 1888, first gained fame in 1920 with his *Proceso histórico del Uruguay*. In 1967, when Arca Press brought out the second printing of the fifth edition of this classic, it became evident that Zum Felde is perhaps the widest read Uruguayan writer of the 1960's. Among his dozen major works, his *Proceso intelec-*

tual del Uruguay, first published in 1930, in its second edition in 1940, became one of the most widely distributed books in Uruguay and in South America, from Montevideo to Buenos Aires to Santiago to Bogotá.

Carlos Quijano, publisher and editor of the weekly news magazine *Marcha,* has been described by Philip B. Taylor as "the most caustic and informed commentator of all Uruguayans."* From 1946 to 1950, Quijano was a leader of the *Demócratas,* an offshoot of the Independent Blancos, nominal conservatives. In the 1960's, Quijano has been a militant leftist, but has written social commentary that has at times shown political independence, depending on the issue. His *Marcha* articles are widely discussed among students, politicians, and civic leaders of the nation.

Luis Carlos Benvenuto, whose writing skill popularizes economics, stirred considerable discussion among Uruguayans in 1967 with his *Breve historia del Uruguay,* giving them an easy-to-read and concise economic history of their nation, which showed that prosperity had once seemed the norm and that the republic still had the resources to solve its crisis of inflation of the 1960's.

Another economist, Enrique Iglesias, director of the Central Bank since that government entity came into being in 1967 under the 1966 constitution, also has gained stature as a writer, with books such as *Uruguay: una propuesta de cambio.* In his brief books, Iglesias puts the prevailing economic trends into everyday language, in a manner similar to that of syndicated columnist Sylvia Porter in the United States.

A playwright, Carlos Maggi, has gained fame as a humorist with his book *El Uruguay y su gente,* originally published in 1963 and in its second edition in 1965. His book *Gardel, Onetti y algo más,* a tongue-in-cheek look at the tango and folklore culture, was Uruguay's best seller in 1964 and is still being reprinted. In 1962, Maggi wrote a motion picture scenario, *La raya amarilla,* which

* Philip B. Taylor, *Government and Politics of Uruguay* (New Orleans, La.: Tulane Studies in Political Science, 1960), p. 23.

he then directed as a short film, which won a prize at the International Film Festival at Brussels. Maggi's quips about Uruguay's not having jungles or wild animals or exotic Indians to attract tourists are often heard within scripts of television programs in Montevideo.

THE PRESS

Uruguay's newspapers have long had an impact on public life. In this highly literate nation, the daily newspapers of Montevideo have offered citizens meaningful discussion of public issues for decades and have reflected the social and economic trends of the republic. With the exception of a brief period in 1933, Uruguay has not suffered any press censorship since 1904, and the vigor of its mass media reflects this freedom.

Uruguay, however, did suffer a lengthy press strike in 1967, from July 1 to October 24. For 117 days, nine of the eleven daily newspapers of Montevideo did not appear. The three newspaper unions — for reporters-editors, for printers-engravers, and for street vendors — wanted a 40 per cent pay increase, inasmuch as the cost of living had risen 36.5 per cent during the first half of 1967. So, on the surface, the 40 per cent pay hike seemed in line. But the unions were not talking about a July 1 base but, rather, a January 1 base, or a 76.5 per cent increase in salaries that publishers would have to meet. Finally, a government conciliator got labor and management talking in realistic terms. The October settlement consisted of a 35 per cent pay boost, based on July 1 salaries.

For almost four months, every morning the only local daily in Montevideo was *El Popular,* organ of FIdeL, whose normal circulation of 3,000 rose to 15,000. Every evening, the only Montevideo daily was *Extra,* a tabloid that escaped the stoppage because it had been founded only a few months before and therefore enjoyed a new-contract status. *Extra* publisher Carlos Fraschini supported the Gestido administration and, subsequently, the Pacheco administration.

Dean of the Uruguayan press is another tabloid filled with color photography, *BP Color*. It was founded in 1878 as *El Bien Público* by Juan Zorrilla de San Martín, as the voice of the Civic Union, which evolved into the Christian Democratic Party. After *El Bien Público* went bankrupt in 1963, it was revived as *BP Color,* its former literary style being replaced by features aimed at a mass audience.

Though neither the oldest nor the largest newspaper of Uruguay, *El Día* remains pre-eminent because it was founded by José Batlle in 1886 and, ever since, has reflected significant Colorado thought on major issues, as well as serving as an accurate record of events through professional reporting and editing. Its circulation of 65,000 reaches most of the political and civic leaders of the nation, all the libraries, and most of the school administrators and similar persons influential in shaping public opinion.

In the 1940's and 1950's, *El Día* was controlled closely by the three sons and two daughters of José Batlle. In the late 1960's, Jorge Luis Franzini began to dominate the paper as executive publisher. In 1964 he modernized its appearance by removing classified and display advertisements from the front page, in favor of a readable page of news stories.

For twenty-five years, Hugo Fernández Artucio was political editor of *El Día,* until the 1966 presidential campaign. The noted journalist and educator supported Oscar Gestido, whereas the paper editorially supported the Colorado faction favoring retention of the plural presidency originated by the famous founder of *El Día. El Día's* executive editor, Jorge Pacheco Areco, remained friendly with the newspaper, although he too left it to campaign as Gestido's running mate, succeeding to the presidency himself in December, 1967.

The Colorado faction Unity and Reform (List 15), founded in 1946 by Luis Batlle, has its editorial voice in *Acción,* the daily that he established in 1948. After this former president died in 1964, his son, Jorge Batlle, became publisher of *Acción.* Luis Hierro Gambardella was political editor of *Acción* until he was elected a senator in November, 1966. Then, in 1967, he served four months as minister of culture under President Gestido before returning to the Senate. Like *El Día, Acción* has given some editorial comfort to the Gestido and Pacheco administrations.

Still another supporter of the Colorados is the daily *La Mañana,* founded in 1917 by Pedro Manini Ríos and now owned by his son Carlos. When he joined the Gestido cabinet in 1967, Carlos Manini Ríos took a leave of absence from the paper, and continued it in 1968 as head of the Bank of the Republic. In his absence, Raúl Blengio Brito has been *Mañana* publisher.

Mañana's afternoon affiliate, *El Diario,* has the largest circulation of any newspaper in the republic, selling more than 100,000 copies daily. Editorially it too supports the Colorado Party, sometimes strongly but most often with a degree of independence. Founded in 1917, *El Diario* has furnished a balanced roundup of economic and political news, sports stories, and human-interest features. Despite its large circulation, it does not seem to have the political impact that *El Día* or *Acción* have.

A prominent editorial voice of the National Party, *El Debate* was founded in 1931 by the most famous of all Blancos, Luis Alberto de Herrera. With Wáshington Guadalupe as executive publisher and editor, *El Debate* in the 1960's has been shaped politically by its political editor, Martín R. Echegoyen, who was 1966 presidential candidate of the Nationalist Popular Movement after it broke away from the Blanco Democratic Union (UBD) faction of the National Party. A senator and a presiding officer of the legislature, Echegoyen became a leader of the *Herrerista* sector of the Blancos in the 1950's and served on the National Council of Government when the Blanco majority came to power, during the 1959–65 term of the plural presidency.

In the 1930's and 1940's, *El Debate* kept its ultraconservative image politically by editorially supporting Franco in Spain and Perón in Argentina. In the 1960's, its political emphasis has been more toward economic questions. Another writer for *Debate* prominent in Blanco politics has been Eduardo Víctor Haedo, a member of the National Council of Government during 1959–63 and a senator during 1963–67. A political editor for *El Debate,* Carlos M. Penades helped found the UBD faction of the National Party, then became a supporter of Martín Echegoyen. A member of the National Council of Government, Penades served as a senator during 1959–63 and is again serving during the 1967–72 term. His senatorial duties keep him from much active work with the paper.

El País, founded in 1918, a morning daily with a circulation of 60,000, has been moderately conservative politically and hence has enjoyed the broad appeal among Blancos that *El Día* has had among Colorados. Until the Blanco Democratic Union was formed in 1956 as a major National Party faction, *El País* supported the Independent Nationalists. Then, one of the paper's owners and editors, Wáshington Beltrán, oriented *El País* politically toward the UBD. Beltrán, a member of the National Council of Government during 1963–67 and a senator during 1967–72, has given the Blancos some literary luster and an image of political glamor through his writing for *El País.*

The afternoon affiliate of *El País* is *El Plata,* founded in 1914. Under publisher José Antonio Ramírez, its editorial policies parallel those of *El País.* Adolfo Tejera, one of the founders of the UBD, has been a writer for *El Plata.* Tejera served as minister of the interior in 1964–65, as a senator before that, and as a board director for the government-owned ANCAP. As a diplomat at the United Nations and as an ANCAP official, Tejera tended to emphasize moderately conservative policies in the columns of *El Plata,* whose staff he formally left in 1963, having originally become affiliated with the paper in 1937.

The building housing *El País* and *El Plata* faces Plaza Libertad in downtown Montevideo, at Kilometer Zero, in the strategic center of the city, four blocks from the presidential palace at Plaza de Independencia. A little to the north, on 18 de Julio Avenue, *El Día*'s building enjoys the second best-centralized location of all the newspaper plants.

North American and British residents have a semiweekly newspaper *The Montevidean,* published and edited by Mrs. Ilma

Lewis. Each Wednesday and Saturday, it tells them about social club, church, school, and other Anglo-American community affairs, with some brief foreign and national news stories. *L'Ora D'Italia*, Montevideo's Italian-language newspaper, comes out only every other week, though more than one-fourth of all Uruguayans are of Italian, rather than Spanish or Portuguese, descent. Despite Italian surnames, many Uruguayans whose grandfathers came from Italy, themselves are completely assimilated into Hispanic society. With Buenos Aires across the Plata estuary, several prominent Argentine daily newspapers also sell in Montevideo.

Montevideo's daily newspapers also serve as national publications, reaching subscribers in the nineteen departmental capitals, plus the other cities of the nation. Yet, despite the prominence of the Montevideo newspapers all over Uruguay, the interior of the republic does support eighteen daily newspapers, thirty-nine weekly newspapers, and twenty-nine other newspapers coming out twice a month or monthly. The combined circulation of these eighty-six papers totals 115,600, compared with almost 300,000 for the Montevideo press. Most of the leading writers of Uruguay from time to time do pen articles for one or more of the Montevideo daily newspapers, but almost never for the provincial press.

BROADCASTING

Radio broadcasting came to the republic as a daily service in 1922. In 1921 the General Electric company set up an experimental twenty-watt transmitter in the Urquiza Theater, at the corner of Mercedes and Andes streets, where today the Radio Sodre studios are located. The following year, Sebastián Paradizábal, a Montevideo merchant, bought the experimental station and hired Claudio Sapelli as engineer and Luis Viapianna, a popular young singer, as an announcer, to broadcast commercials and entertainment on a regular daily basis to promote his retail store.

The Ministry of Commerce issued a license to Radio Paradizábal as of mid-1922, although no basic broadcast law yet existed.

Station CW 35, or Radio Paysandú, received the first license with the label "commercial broadcasting" on May 25, 1924. On December 24, 1924, Radio Monte Carlo received the second commercial license; today it is one of the leading stations of the republic and the oldest one still operating. On November 1, 1922, the former president of Uruguay José Batlle, introduced by Luis Viapianna, spoke into a Radio Paradizábal microphone for a half hour, the first chief executive to address the nation by radio.

Radio Sodre, the government's own station, in 1930 considered selling air time to defray the cost of remote pickups for popular soccer match broadcasts. But, once the economy began to recover from economic depression, Sodre relinquished commercial announcements to the privately owned stations. Only in the late 1950's, when Sodre's television outlet, Channel 5, went into daily service, did the government broadcasting company again send out air-time salesmen, for television only, not for radio.

Television broadcasting did not come to Uruguay until December 7, 1956, when the republic's first station, Channel 10, affiliated with Radio Carve, went on the air. The other three television stations of Montevideo, with audiences all over the republic, are Sodre's television outlet; Channel 4, an affiliate of the veteran Radio Monte Carlo; and Channel 12. The capital's four television stations send clear signals into homes on the Brazilian and Argentine borders.

In the 1960's some of the leading young writers of Uruguay have explored the medium of television, scripting dramas, documentaries, and variety programs. One skilled news commentator, Eduardo Huertas, has brought to the Montevideo screen some narration and description that compares favorably with similar programs in the United States.

Any public controversy, no matter how shocking to traditionalists, can get a hearing somewhere on the air in Uruguay—if not on the television channels always, then on one or more of the radio stations. The progressive political climate of Uruguay for decades has prepared the listening public to weigh the merits and demerits of almost any issue, from problems of sexual abnormalities to rock music.

All four of Uruguay's television stations depend on cigarette advertising for part of their revenues, yet these stations, almost alone among Latin American video outlets, have not lacked the courage to run panel discussions on the harmful effects of smoking. Channel 5 acquainted Uruguayans with the U.S. Surgeon General's report on the danger of lung cancer from cigarette smoking, the first broadcasting station in the hemisphere outside the United States and Canada to air such a documentary program. With typical Uruguayan candidness, not only the government channel, but also the three commercial television stations from time to time have turned a documentary spotlight on the danger to health from smoking, alcoholism, poor dietary habits, and inadequate personal hygiene.

Of the twenty-two Montevideo radio stations, only six have genuine news departments, with teletype printers from one or more of the world-wide news agencies and one or more professionally trained newsmen to gather and edit local stories. Montevideo's leading radio stations have provincial affiliates, which receive news reports via network hookups.

Radio Carve, owned and operated by Raúl Fontaina, former president of the Inter-American Broadcasters Association, has the only Associated Press full-time wire service among the radio stations. One of Fontaina's sons manages the affiliated television station, Channel 10, and another son has served as a member of the legislature.

Radio El Espectador, whose capable news department stresses national affairs, maintains reporters in the press gallery of the Senate and the Chamber of Representatives when the General Assembly is in session, as well as a reporter at the office of the president of the republic.

Radio Sarandí, Radio Oriental, and Radio Ariel, with copy from United Press International, Agence France Presse, and the

British news agency Reuter's, give regularly scheduled five-minute news roundups at the beginning of each hour during peak listening periods of the day.

Radio Monte Carlo, which also is among the leading news stations, hooks several provincial stations into its early afternoon roundup of news. Radio Sarandí has affiliated stations in Artigas and Salto, near the Brazilian and Argentine borders, for its one-hour news roundup every morning.

In Uruguay, unlike the United States, the law permits the issuing of a license to an individual or company for two broadcasting stations in the same city. Therefore, the *Dirección General de Telecomunicaciones* (Bureau of Telecommunications), of the Ministry of Communications, Transportation, and Tourism, has issued a license to the parent corporation of Radio El Espectador to operate a second Montevideo radio station, Radio Libertad Sport, whose athletic emphasis is popular in a nation that idolizes soccer players.

Radio-station licenses must be renewed every year, but, as long as transmitting frequencies are not tampered with nor profanity aired, the renewal is automatic upon the filing of a programing summary. Television-station licenses are issued for a ten-year period, and renewal consideration by the Bureau of Telecommunications is much more extensive.

PERFORMING ARTS

Some of the leading actors and actresses of television programs also star on the stage in Montevideo. For example, China Zorrilla, who offers women's interest programs on television, also stars in plays with the Comedia Nacional, a permanent repertory production company housed in the Teatro Solís. Despite its name, the National Comedy company is underwritten by the municipal government of Montevideo, not by the national government, although the Ministry of Culture does have final authority over it.

In a theater operated by the Sodre broadcasting company, both established plays and new offerings by South American play-wrights often alternate. At the Odeon Theater, Shakespeare seasons will alternate with modern dramas. At the Verdi Theater, comedies usually are presented. In the various colleges of the University of the Republic, in secondary schools, at binational cultural centers, on library patios in the suburbs, and in the lounges of civic clubs, various amateur and semiprofessional drama groups also add to the variety of live theater offerings at any one time in Montevideo. Away from the capital, motion picture theaters provide most of the dramatic fare, although some provincial amateur drama groups perform in Salto, Pay-sandú, and a few other cities.

Although Montevideo does not support a permanent profes-sional opera company, many of the internationally famous singers who perform with opera companies at the Teatro Colón in Buenos Aires also schedule performances at the Teatro Solís in Montevideo. The National School of Ballet, operated by the Ministry of Culture, also provides a resident company for visiting ballet stars as well as the local opportunity for semiprofessional ballet groups to perform regularly in Montevideo. Since its inauguration in 1856, the Teatro Solís has provided a national stage for Uruguayan playwrights, such as Samuel Blixen (1869–1909) and Florencio Sánchez (1875–1910). In the 1960's, how-ever, much of the live theater in Uruguay, both dramas and musical reviews, have come from Broadway, London, and Paris in translation, and from Mexico City and Buenos Aires.

In the realm of serious music, Uruguay's best-known composer with an international reputation was Eduardo Fabini, who lived from 1883 to 1951, famed for his symphonies. Héctor Tosar Errecart in the 1950's captured national and international atten-tion as a composer with his neoclassical adaptation of gaucho folk themes in "Danza Criolla." Although the tango is univer-sally thought of as Argentine, the best-known tango of all time, "La Cumparsita," was written by a Uruguayan composer, Gerardo H. Matos Rodríguez.

In 1940, Francisco Curt Lange, one of the leading musicologists in Latin America, founded the *Instituto Americano de Musicología* in Montevideo, with help from the Uruguayan Government. Today, a National Conservatory of Music carries on the high professional level of musicological research that Lange brought to Montevideo.

PAINTING AND SCULPTURE

One of the greatest painters not only in the history of Uruguay but also during this century in most of South America was Pedro Figari, who lived from 1861 to 1938. His vivid studies of Uruguayan life bring high prices in art galleries throughout the Western world. His canvases are immediately recognizable as colorful rural scenes of country families dancing around a campfire or on a patio, seated by a ranch house, listening to a guitarist, or at one of the many harbors or ports of the Uruguay River or the Atlantic seacoast. In the realm of modern art, J. Torres García (1874–1944) gained the most fame among Uruguayan experimental painters in various world galleries.

A leader of the impressionistic artists of Uruguay was the painter Pedro Blanes Viale (1879–1926), whose historical scenes decorate the Legislative Palace. His landscapes hang in the National Museum of Fine Arts in Montevideo, but a few of his works remain in Paris. An earlier Blanes also brought world notice to Uruguay. He was Juan Manuel Blanes (1830–1901), an artist acclaimed by both New World and Old World critics. Blanes' works captured Uruguayan history—"Oath of the Immortal Thirty-Three," "Battle of Sarandí," "Artigas in 1815," and "Assassination of Florencio Varela."

In sculpture, the two most famous statues in Uruguay are the *carreta,* a covered wagon being driven westward by pioneer settlers, by José Belloni, and the gaucho astride a horse, standing guard at the intersection of 18 de Julio and Constituyente avenues, in Montevideo, by José Luis Zorrilla de San Martín, son of the distinguished writer Juan Zorrilla. And Zorrilla also designed the "Last Charrúa" statue of the pre-Spanish Indians of the

Banda Oriental, in Prado Park. In Batlle Park, the Belloni sculpture of the *carreta* probably rates as the single most photographed object in Uruguay, as evidenced by tourist visits and photography displays. Three pair of yoked oxen pull a covered wagon, with a bearded horseman leading two other oxen, as rugged pioneer settlers face toward the western and northern regions where they would establish ranches.

SPORTS

Fishing, swimming, and yachting clubs dot the nation's coast-lines. But the most popular sport in Uruguay is *fútbol* (football), the game called soccer in the United States. Every town in Uruguay has its soccer fields, and every school its young champions hoping to rise to the big-time professional teams. No political rally ever matches the excitement of a gathering of fans of the nation's two leading teams, Peñarol and Nacional.

In 1930, to celebrate the 100th anniversary of the promulgation of the constitution of 1830, the nation's leaders inaugurated the *Estadio Centenario* with a soccer match watched by 100,000 fans. That July 18, the police force had one of its most trying challenges; for most of the 100,000 spectators were Uruguayans, witnessing a Uruguayan team win its first world's soccer championship. No economic or political crisis in the republic's history ever prompted the cacophony of noises, litter of confetti, and absence of any hint of normal business routines that soccer prompts. In 1890, employees of the British Uruguayan Railways organized the Peñarol Club and in 1900 the rival Nacional was established. Ever since, the nation has divided into two camps more adamant than the members of the Colorado and Blanco political parties. In 1967 and 1968, not even the worst strikes nor economic crises could engender as many protestors on the streets as could a close soccer match.

CARNIVAL

During autumn (March, April, May), winter (June, July, August), and spring (September, October, November), soccer games remain in the news. As summer begins, in December, the professional *fútbol* season ends, just in time for Uruguayans to fill the beaches for swimming. Volleyball and basketball tournaments continue all summer. For more than a half century bullfighting has been outlawed and holds no interest for Uruguayans. But another tradition handed down from Latin Europe to Latin America, *Carnaval,* shows no signs of diminishing.

Although Uruguay has become a secular state, the week preceding Lent remains the one Catholic tradition central to the social life of the republic. Even though Lent itself finds few Uruguayans giving up pleasures for penitence, Carnival Week emphasizes the good times that Catholics are supposed to be amassing before the abstinence sets in. A wild atmosphere ensues, just as if the period of Ash Wednesday to Easter Sunday were to be austere. Every club, hotel, and open-air arena houses public dances. Costumes and masks radiate every color of the rainbow. Street parades feature flowered floats, and buildings sport colored lights and paper streamers. Especially exciting are the *tablados,* or special shows.

Each neighborhood in Montevideo, with the financial help of the municipal government, builds a stage facing a street. Across the stage streams the local talent, from musicians to clowns. The Carnivals in Rio de Janeiro and in New Orleans are each better advertised globally. But nowhere in the Latin world does a Carnival exude any more spontaneous joy than in Montevideo. Uruguayans are less formal than Argentines or Peruvians or Chileans anyway. And at Carnival time, they are as rollicking as any people on earth.

IX

Foreign Relations

Uruguay's active role in the United Nations, the Organization of American States (OAS), and the Alliance for Progress in recent decades has made this republic one of the vigorous voices of democracy in international relations. At many of the key gatherings of the nations of the world, Uruguayan diplomats have served in administrative posts with distinction. Uruguay has furnished diplomats to world organizations far out of proportion to its size. In 1968, José A. Mora of Uruguay retired after twelve years of service as secretary-general of the OAS. Another Uruguayan diplomat, Emilio Oribe, during 1968 served as president of the OAS Council.

Ever since the formalizing of Pan Americanism in 1889, Uruguayans have played key roles in inter-American affairs. As a small nation, a buffer wedged between two large countries, Uruguay naturally has favored multinational solutions to disputes; and, as a dedicated democracy, it has encouraged peaceful solutions to quarrels between nations. As an exporter of beef and wool, Uruguay has enjoyed friendly relations with its best customers, such as Britain, Italy, and the United States. Dedicated to its own freedom, Uruguay has been willing to keep its lines of communication open with dictatorships and free lands alike, thereby often serving as a reliable mediator in regional and world disputes.

With its reputation as a democratic force in hemispheric and international organizations, Uruguay has attracted numerous nongovernmental international organizations to its capital. Montevideo is the headquarters for South America for the Young Men's Christian Association and related YMCA groups. Montevideo is also the headquarters for all of Latin America for the feminine counterpart, the Young Women's Christian Association. Under the able direction of Ruth Van Meter, the hemispheric technical council and administrative headquarters of the YWCA coordinates the twenty-eight *Asociaciones Cristianas Femeninas* of Latin America and the Caribbean region.

DIALOGUE WITH DEMOCRACIES

In 1888–89, Uruguay for the first time played host to an international conference, the Congress on Private International Law, in Montevideo. Delegates from Argentina, Bolivia, Brazil, Chile, Paraguay, Peru, and Uruguay negotiated multilateral treaties on international commercial law, civil law, penal law, procedural law, and patents and trademarks.

Extending this 1889 Uruguayan interest in peaceful international relations, no less a delegate than José Batlle y Ordóñez represented Uruguay at the second Hague Conference in 1907. Having finished his first term as president of the republic, Batlle consented to serve as a diplomat to foster the idea of an international court of justice. On July 29, 1907, Batlle addressed the Hague Conference, anticipating by a decade Woodrow Wilson's proposals for the League of Nations. In 1919, the noted Buenos Aires newspaper *La Nación* could point to Batlle's 1907 speech for an international court as a forerunner of proposals at Versailles for the League of Nations.

Uruguay became a charter member of the League of Nations. Among its distinguished diplomats serving on key league committees was Alberto Guani, later foreign minister and vice-president of Uruguay in the 1940's. From 1923 to 1926, Uruguay served as a member of the Council of the League of Nations, often taking the lead in action to promote arbitration among nations and relief measures for children and the aged. The first international conference of the League of Nations to meet in Latin America convened in Montevideo in 1927, to plan public-health programs to lessen infant mortality.

Paralleling its work for international cooperation, Uruguay also stressed good inter-American relations. During 1889–90, in Washington, the Pan American Union had launched the inter-American security system, with conferences in Mexico City in 1902, in Rio de Janeiro in 1906, and in Buenos Aires in 1910. In June, 1917, Uruguay's foreign minister proclaimed that "no American country, which, in defense of its own rights, finds itself in a state of war with nations of other continents, will be treated as a belligerent." Uruguay thereupon repealed all neutrality laws so far as the United States, Brazil, Cuba, and Panama were concerned, these powers being at war with Germany.

This 1917 declaration of inter-American solidarity was a forerunner of a principle formalized in 1947, that aggression against any Western Hemisphere nation should be considered aggression against all the republics of the hemisphere. Then, in April, 1920, Uruguayan President Baltasar Brum called for a "League of Nations of North, Central, and South America," based on equality among the Latin American republics and the United States. In 1948 this Brum concept became reality, when the old interAmerican system was chartered as the OAS.

In the 1920's, Uruguay played a prominent role in inter-American affairs. In 1929, and from 1935 to 1938, Uruguay coordinated the Pan American Commission of Neutrals, to conciliate the Chaco War between Bolivia and Paraguay. The Fifth and Sixth Inter-American conferences—at Santiago in 1923 and at Havana in 1928—were especially negative, reflecting Latin American resentment of U.S. policies in Nicaragua, Haiti, the Dominican Republic, and Panama. But, when Montevideo played host to the Seventh Inter-American Conference in 1933, the atmosphere had changed. This Uruguayan meeting became known as the Good Neighbor Conference.

In his March, 1933, inaugural address, U.S. President Franklin

D. Roosevelt had pledged his foreign policy to be that of a good neighbor. At Montevideo, when the Inter-American Conference convened, U.S. Secretary of State Cordell Hull emphasized that U.S. Latin American policy now centered in nonintervention in the internal affairs of other nations.

As host, Uruguayan diplomats worked diligently to get other Latin American delegates to support the new position of the United States, and to ignore the hostile position of Argentina, which seemingly wanted to keep alive old suspicions. At the close of the conference, a treaty on the rights and duties of states cited the equality among nations, large and small; the inviolability of national territory; and a determination of hemispheric republics not to recognize the results of armed force as equivalent to peaceful means for bringing about political change. Caught up in the Good Neighbor theme, the various delegations signed this treaty.

As World War II raged in Europe, after September 1, 1939, Uruguay and other Latin American nations became concerned about Axis ships bringing the fighting to their doorsteps. On December 12 and December 13, 1939, the German battleship *Graf Spee* and the British cruisers *Ajax, Achilles,* and *Exeter* engaged in a running battle off the coast of Uruguay. After British guns badly damaged the *Graf Spee,* it sought refuge in the harbor of Montevideo.

In accordance with international law, the Uruguayan foreign minister ordered the German warship to leave national waters. After protests, the *Graf Spee* left. To avoid capture by the British on the high seas, the ship scuttled itself just outside Montevideo harbor. Nazi anger with Uruguay for this humiliation culminated in a German plot in 1940 to overthrow the government in Montevideo, replacing it with a Nazi puppet regime. In mid-1940, the Uruguayan legislature confirmed the plot, which news editor Hugo Fernández Artucio of *El Día* had uncovered. Uruguayan public opinion surged overwhelmingly for the Allies.

In June, 1941, the Uruguayan president announced that the

ports of his nation would be available to the navies of any Western Hemisphere republic that became a belligerent in the war. Uruguay thereupon constructed a large naval air base near its Brazilian border and expanded Punta del Este port facilities to handle warships.

FROM WARTIME ALLY TO U.N. FOUNDING MEMBER

After the United States entered the war on December 8, 1941, President Alfredo Baldomir and Foreign Minister Alberto Guani promptly declared Uruguayan solidarity with the Allies. Supplementing (and later supplanting) the regular inter-American conferences, the foreign ministers' meetings of the inter-American system began in September, 1939, in Panama, to face the problem of neutrality in World War II.

At the Third Inter-American Foreign Ministers Meeting in Rio de Janeiro in January, 1942, Uruguay joined several other Latin American nations in breaking diplomatic relations with Germany, Italy, and Japan. This meeting authorized an Emergency Committee for Political Defense, with its headquarters in Montevideo. Uruguayan Foreign Minister Guani became committee chairman, continuing in that post after he became vice-president of Uruguay late in 1942. Uruguay formally declared war on the Axis powers on February 15, 1945, although this nation had no large military forces to send overseas. Diplomatically and economically, Uruguay already had been fighting for the Allies in ways that the democratic republic knew best: Axis agents had been arrested and pro-Axis broadcasts from Buenos Aires were answered by Montevideo stations.

In May, 1945, in San Francisco, Uruguay became a charter member of the United Nations. The chairman of the Uruguayan delegation was José Serrato, who had been president of the republic during 1923–27. As the United Nations began to develop in New York, during 1945–47, Uruguayan delegates Nector Payseé Reyes and José A. Mora lent their diplomatic skill to making the Latin American bloc of nations an influential voice.

As a U.N. member, Uruguay supported the decision of the world organization to oppose North Korean troops' moving into South Korea in 1950. In November, 1950, Uruguay formally appropriated $2 million to aid the U.N. forces in Korea. Uruguayan blankets and other woolen products helped comfort the South Korean victims of the fighting.

Throughout the 1950's and 1960's, Uruguay became an active leader in UNESCO, the U.N. Educational, Scientific, and Cultural Organization. In 1954, Montevideo was host for the general meeting of UNESCO; and, in 1960, Uruguayans helped plan a meeting in Quito to further vocational training.

INTER-AMERICAN RELATIONS

On November 22, 1945, Uruguayan Foreign Minister Eduardo Rodríguez Larreta proposed to U.S. Secretary of State James F. Byrnes that the republics of the Americas adopt the policy of collective intervention if one of the hemisphere's nations violated its international obligations or the basic rights of man. At the time, Argentina was suffering the first stages of the dictatorship of Juan Perón, which would last until September, 1955. During the Perón era, Uruguay served as a symbol of hope for Argentines suffering censorship, imprisonment, police torture, exile, or other loss of basic liberties. Radio broadcasts from Montevideo became the source of authentic news to Argentines beset with propaganda and government-managed "information."

In 1947, in Rio de Janeiro, at a special inter-American conference, Uruguay enthusiastically joined the other nations of the hemisphere in signing the Inter-American Treaty of Reciprocal Assistance, known as the Rio Treaty. The treaty stipulates that an armed attack by any nation upon a Western Hemisphere nation shall be considered an attack against all the other nations. Consultation would determine the nature of the collective action to be taken.

The principle of the Rio Treaty became a cornerstone of the OAS, which grew out of the former Pan American Union, and whose charter was formally signed in Bogotá in 1948. On January 19, 1956, the OAS Council elected José A. Mora as interim secretary-general and, later, to a full ten-year term beginning in May, 1958. On May 18, 1968, José A. Mora completed his ten-year term as secretary-general of the OAS. The veteran Uruguayan diplomat had been the third secretary-general since the older inter-American system, built around the Pan American Union, had been modernized in 1948.

Mora had been the only secretary-general to serve the OAS for a full ten-year term. The first secretary-general, Alberto Lleras Camargo, served eight years, during 1946–54, resigning to return to his native Colombia to help end civil strife and to serve as president of that republic during 1958–62, then becoming publisher of one of Latin America's leading news magazines, *Visión*. The second secretary-general, Carlos Dávila of Chile, served from 1954 until his death from a heart attack on October 19, 1955.

The New York Times on January 21, 1956, referred to Mora's role as one of the "most sensitive posts in the Western Hemisphere. Of all the regional organizations of the world, the OAS is the most successful in the peaceful settlement of disputes and the Secretary General always plays a key role when trouble arises." During 1945–47, Mora had served as a representative of Uruguay at the United Nations and, from 1948 on, was Uruguayan ambassador to the OAS and, simultaneously, Uruguayan ambassador to the United States. In January, 1956, just before being chosen as OAS secretary-general, Mora still held both posts simultaneously. At that time, Luis Batlle Berres, as president of the National Council of Government of Uruguay, paid a state visit to the United States. Realizing that few men had the energy to fill both posts, Batlle recommended that Uruguay have a top diplomat in each post.

From its early years as a buffer between Argentina and Brazil to its role in this century as a catalytic agent for hemispheric peace and cooperation, Uruguay has consistently maintained its dialogue with democracies. In 1960, at the Sixth Inter-American

Foreign Ministers Meeting in San José, Costa Rica, the OAS decided to condemn the Trujillo dictatorship of the Dominican Republic by recalling ambassadors and suspending trade relations. Trujillo had attempted to have the president of Venezuela killed.

Also, in August, 1960, in San José, the Seventh Inter-American Foreign Ministers Meeting dealt with the Castro dictatorship in Cuba. But it remained for the Eighth Inter-American Foreign Ministers Meeting at Punta del Este, Uruguay, in 1962, for the OAS to deal strongly with Castro. This Punta del Este meeting voted to exclude the Castro administration from participating in the inter-American system and to suspend armaments trade with Cuba.

The Ninth Inter-American Foreign Ministers Meeting, in Washington, in 1964, was called by Venezuela to deal with charges of Cuban terrorism against the Caracas government. As in 1960 and 1962, in 1964 Uruguay supported the democratic Venezuelan Government, voting to condemn the Cuban Government for sending guerrillas and terrorists into Venezuela.

THE ALLIANCE FOR PROGRESS AND THE COMMON MARKET

In 1958, Brazilian President Juscelino Kubitschek proposed Operation Pan America, a hemispheric effort to expand the economies of the Latin American nations so that standards of living would rise and the danger of undemocratic governments would lessen. Following up that line of thinking, the OAS Council convened on April 8, 1959, in Washington, to sign the agreement establishing the Inter-American Development Bank. During 1959–60, the first steps toward a Central American common market were taken. In 1960, the Act of Bogotá resolved hemispheric reforms in tax structures and, in February, 1960, in Uruguay, the Treaty of Montevideo was signed, creating the Latin American Free Trade Association (LAFTA).

LAFTA's headquarters are in Montevideo, where the economic representatives of the member nations work toward extending

LAFTA into a genuine Latin American common market. At its 1960 founding, LAFTA had seven members: Argentina, Brazil, Chile, Mexico, Paraguay, Peru, and Uruguay. In 1961, Colombia and Ecuador joined and, in 1967, Venezuela and Bolivia boosted the total to eleven members.

According to the Treaty of Montevideo, LAFTA members annually negotiate reduced tariffs on selected imports until each nation's tariff level has been cut 8 per cent. In addition, a second list is drawn up every three years, onto which each LAFTA member must put a group of products representing 25 per cent of the intrazonal trade for the previous three years. Items on this second list will be free-traded throughout the region starting in 1973. The annual lists for reduced tariffs were agreed upon readily. But the three-year compilations engendered considerable debate at Bogotá, in 1964, and at the Seventh General Session of LAFTA at Montevideo during November and December, 1967.

With LAFTA headquarters in Montevideo working strenuously throughout the year, the Treaty of Montevideo has increased intraregional trade each year since 1960, with 60 per cent of this trade being in raw materials and processed products for industry, 22 per cent in fuels and lubricants, and 11 per cent in nondurable consumer goods.

With LAFTA as a tangible beginning and the Inter-American Development Bank as the catalytic agent for economic growth, the inter-American system by 1961 seemed ready for a formal program for hemispheric economic growth. The United States appeared to be prepared to update and broaden its foreign policy in Latin America; and Uruguay indicated that it was eager to host a conference translating into action the broad principles of Operation Pan America.

On March 13, 1961, U.S. President John F. Kennedy announced that U.S. foreign aid would emphasize development loans to Latin American nations at low or zero interest rates, with $1 billion to be pledged within one year. The ideas of Operation Pan America, the Treaty of Montevideo, and the Inter-American

Development Bank would all come under the terms of the Alliance for Progress, in which the nations of the hemisphere would cooperate for economic growth and political health. Tax reforms would stimulate private sectors of the economies, resulting in new payrolls. Governmental commitment to social justice would engender reforms to reduce illiteracy, poverty, and the social conditions that encourage the political paths of least resistance, culminating in dictatorships.

From August 5 to August 17, 1961, at Punta del Este, Uruguay hosted the economic and finance ministers of the OAS, who finalized and signed the charter of the Alliance for Progress. Uruguayan Minister of Finance Juan Eduardo Azzini served as conference chairman. The United States and all the Latin American nations except Cuba signed the charter and the Declaration of Punta del Este, which asserted that "This Alliance is established on the basic principle that free men working through the institution of representative democracy can best satisfy man's aspirations, including those for work, home, land, health, and schools." Both the declaration and the charter called for a 2.5 per cent annual per capita increase in the economic growth of the nations of the Americas.

The Uruguayan delegation, with Héctor Lorenzo Lozada as its chairman, worked to get the Punta del Este delegates to study the need for a common market in hemispheric efforts at economic growth. Uruguay's delegation collided head-on with the Cuban delegation, led by Communist leader Ernesto "Ché" Guevara, who at the time was Cuban minister of industry.

The Uruguayan National Council of Government utilized police, student groups, anti-Communist labor groups, and educators to keep the Cubans from disrupting the conference. When a small group of Communist students organized a demonstration against U.S. Secretary of the Treasury C. Douglas Dillon, a larger, anti-Communist student group showed up to applaud the efforts of the United States in an inter-American partnership. U.N. economist Raúl Prebisch and President of the Inter-American Development Bank Felipe Herrera termed the Punta del Este gathering "one of Uruguay's finest hours" of hosting a conference to a harmonious conclusion. Juan de Onís, *The New York Times* correspondent, described the speeches as being "full of revolutionary boldness, frank self-criticism, and practical proposals." Another noted *New York Times* correspondent, Tad Szulc, reported, on August 18, 1961, that the Punta del Este atmosphere linked representative government to economic progress.

During April 12–14, 1967, also in Punta del Este, Uruguay hosted a conference of the presidents of the nations of the OAS. A resolution called for a Latin American common market by 1985. The chief executives pledged support for the electric power, highway, and communications network needed to build a large common market and to make it competitive in world trade.

Uruguayan President Oscar Gestido and Foreign Minister Héctor Luisi at the 1967 summit meeting at Punta del Este radiated the same spirit of hemispheric cooperation evidenced at the Montevideo LAFTA meeting in 1960 and at the Alliance for Progress chartering in 1961. Gestido did not realize that eight months later he would pass on, leaving the Uruguayan Government in the hands of Vice-President Jorge Pacheco. Yet, providentially, Gestido included Pacheco in most of the major meetings that April, thereby preparing Pacheco to carry on the Gestido commitment for inter-American economic progress based on common market integration for the hemisphere.

In 1968, the Inter-American Committee of the Alliance for Progress (CIAP) began to refer to the "spirit of Punta del Este," as national development programs of various Latin American nations began to give evidence of economic reforms indicating better allocation of resources, reflecting the general blueprint of the Alliance for Progress.

TRADE AND TROUBLE WITH COMMUNIST COUNTRIES

Uruguay has maintained diplomatic and trade relations with most of the nations of the world. Thus, Uruguay maintained full diplomatic relations with the tyrannical Czarist regime in Russia. After the 1917 Bolshevik Revolution, the Banda Oriental pondered whether to resume relations with Russia, and decided to wait until the government in Moscow could speak for the Soviet Union on more than a temporary basis. After a token amount of trade with the U.S.S.R., in 1926 Uruguay became the first Latin American nation to extend full diplomatic recognition to the Soviet Union.

Shortly after opening its Montevideo legation, the U.S.S.R. began using its diplomatic offices as the Communist propaganda center for Latin America. Nine years later, on December 27, 1935, Uruguay broke diplomatic relations with the Soviet Union, after Brazilian President Getúlio Vargas furnished the Uruguayan Foreign Ministry with documentation that Soviet diplomats from Montevideo had been organizing Brazilians in subversive activities. Four days after the diplomatic break, V. M. Molotov, Soviet delegate to the League of Nations, protested to that body that Uruguay had violated the League of Nations Covenant by cutting relations on unproven charges and that the real reason behind the action was Soviet refusal to buy Uruguayan cheese. Four years later, in 1939, Uruguay vigorously participated in the expulsion of the Soviet Union from the League of Nations.

In the 1930's, Argentine Communist leaders Orestes Ghioldi and Victorio Codovilla tried to meddle in Uruguayan politics. When the South American secretariat of the Comintern was established in Buenos Aires, Uruguayan irritation with both the Soviet Union and Argentina increased. However, events during World War II changed the feeling toward the U.S.S.R. to one of sympathy for an ally against the Axis.

In terms of formal relations with the Soviet Union and other Communist nations, Uruguay's wartime cooperation did not give way to cold war aloofness until the dramatic events of 1948, when the Soviet Union blockaded West Berlin, forcing the beleaguered city to be fed by airlift. Two years later, when the Korean conflict erupted, the Uruguayan Government and press again reflected the disapproval of Soviet policies that was felt by many Uruguayans. In 1950, the Uruguayan delegation at the United Nations proposed that international aggression be defined to include "subversive agencies in foreign countries trying to undermine institutions."

The Russian news agency TASS had long maintained a news bureau in Montevideo. Since 1961, the Cuban news service *Prensa Latina* and the Communist Chinese agency New China News have also maintained news bureaus in Montevideo. In recent years, these bureaus have been careful not to involve themselves directly with demonstrations or the distribution of propaganda literature.

In 1957, a TASS correspondent, Mikhail Busivski, had prevented a Soviet diplomat, Ivan Kuznetsov, at gunpoint, from seeking asylum in the Colombian Embassy. Kuznetsov, who was held prisoner in the newsman's house, was returned to Moscow under Soviet guard. A thorough probing by Uruguayan reporters and members of the General Assembly revealed that Busivski had been a member of the U.S.S.R. secret police. The Uruguayan foreign minister informed TASS that its bureau must be staffed by bona fide newsmen if the agency was to remain open in Montevideo.

Despite periods of coolness in the field of diplomacy, in trade relations Uruguay and the Soviet Union in the 1940's and 1950's became better customers. In the early 1940's, Uruguay did only modest trading with the U.S.S.R., whereas neighboring Argentina became the first Latin American nation to develop a significant volume of trade with the entire Soviet bloc. The actions in Buenos Aires to some extent influenced Montevideo, for both Argentina and Uruguay tend to market their meat and hides in a similar manner.

In the late 1950's, Uruguay had begun to feel the effect of lower world prices for wool and took the opportunity to sell more of its exports to Communist nations. Its level of trade with the Soviet Union and the Eastern European Communist nations rose from 5 per cent of Uruguay's total foreign commerce in the early 1950's to 16 per cent in 1958 and 1959, two years when the Soviet Union itself purchased substantial quantities of Uruguayan wool.

By 1959, the non-Communist nations of Europe and Asia, as well as North America, had a shortage of foreign exchange and a surplus of wool supplies. In 1958, Uruguay had become so short of hard-currency reserves that it momentarily shifted substantial portions of its petroleum imports from Western nations to the Soviet Union, which accepted barter in place of bank reserves. In 1959, however, the Uruguayan Government had become concerned enough over the trend to discourage openly Soviet efforts to further increase trade. Uruguay began to change its petroleum imports back to U.S., British, and Canadian companies.

In 1960, the U.S.S.R. tried to force more Uruguayan trade in petroleum; upon receiving another refusal, the Soviet Union abruptly stopped buying any wool from Uruguay. Following the Moscow line, the Eastern European Communist nations reduced their trade with Uruguay to where less than 10 per cent of Uruguayan foreign commerce remained with Soviet bloc nations. Throughout the 1960's, Uruguayan trade with the Soviet Union continued to decline. In 1962, Uruguayan trade with the U.S.S.R. and other Communist nations totaled $24.2 million. By 1964 it had been reduced to $11.2 million, of which only $3.8 million was with the Soviet Union itself.

After the rise to power of Castro in Cuba, the Soviet Communist Party began to send delegates to Communist Party congresses in various Latin American republics. In July, 1962, when the Communist Party of Uruguay convened its Eighteenth Congress, Moscow indicated that this party represented an important unit overseas, helpful to Soviet foreign policies. Four delegates from the Soviet Communist Party were dispatched to the Montevideo meeting. In 1966, the Uruguayan Communist Party held its Nineteenth Congress, but the party had become part of the FIdeL, the Leftist Liberty Front, and no high-ranking Russians spoke this time.

In 1967, Rodney Arismendi, Uruguayan Communist Party secretary-general, stated that, without the support of the Soviet Union, his party might have been forced out of existence, "leaving the workers without a vigorous champion during their oppression by ruinous inflation." In 1968, Arismendi's group continued to encourage strikes, which pushed up wages and prices, thereby continuing that inflationary spiral. In October, 1968, Uruguay expelled three administrators of the Soviet Embassy in Montevideo for interfering in Uruguayan industrial strikes.

During the decade of the 1950's, the official position of the Uruguayan Government and the unofficial posture of its citizens usually made a successful distinction between the intrigues of the Soviet Union and the legitimate grievances of the downtrodden Latin American masses, the victims of decades or centuries of inequities. Just after the Hungarian revolt against the Soviet Union was crushed with tanks in 1956, a professional public-opinion poll was taken of a representative cross section of Uruguayans. The *Instituto Uruguayo de la Opinión Pública* found that only 6 per cent of those interviewed thought that the Soviet Union was not a genuine danger to the free world.

On January 1, 1959, Fidel Castro and his 26th of July rebel movement took over the government from dictator Fulgencio Batista in Cuba. During Castro's first year in office, his repeated vows of faith in democracy engendered sympathy for the Cuban Revolution, for the island republic had long suffered corruption and military-backed dictatorship.

The Uruguayan Government was aware of the changes taking place in the Cuban Revolution, however. In January, 1961, the Cuban Ambassador to Uruguay, Mario García Incháustegui, and the First Secretary of the Soviet Embassy, Mikhail K. Samilov, were declared *personae non gratae* by the National Council of Government. The Uruguayan Foreign Ministry charged both the Cuban diplomat and the Russian diplomat with subversive activities. The January, 1961, report of the ministry contained details of the activities of Soviet Embassy and Cuban Embassy employees at union meetings where strike votes were being taken, at protest gatherings by students during the 1960 visit of U.S. President Eisenhower to South American capitals, and at meetings of every recognized political party of the republic.

Samilov, reportedly the head of a Communist network for subversion throughout Latin America, was described in Uruguayan Foreign Ministry reports as the principal link between Latin America and the Kremlin. Montevideo newspapers considered him more important in the Soviet Embassy in Montevideo than the Soviet Ambassador himself, Sergei S. Mihailov.

In January, 1961, the nine-member National Council of Government began to debate the possibility of breaking relations with Cuba. Five of the nine Council members were against an outright break but did favor joint action against Cuba, to be taken with the other nations of the OAS. Four Council members favored an immediate break in relations with Cuba. That action would come in three and one-half years, after the Eighth Inter-American Foreign Ministers Meeting of the OAS in 1962 and the Ninth in 1964, both of which dealt with the problem of Cuba.

In January, 1962, at Punta del Este, Uruguay hosted the Eighth Inter-American Foreign Ministers Meeting, to deal specifically with the attempts by armed rebels and propaganda agents from Cuba to foment insurrection in other Latin American nations. On the evening before the conference convened, Uruguayan Chargé d'Affaires in Havana Emilio Oribe (who in 1968 as an OAS ambassador would head the OAS Council) presented details on Cuban activities in Latin America. When the vote came, Uruguay joined the majority to exclude Cuba from participating in any OAS activities.

In July, 1964, the Ninth Inter-American Foreign Ministers Meeting met in Washington, to condemn the Cuban Government for engaging in terrorist activities in oil-rich Venezuela. On September 8, 1964, the National Council of Government voted to break Uruguay's diplomatic relations with Cuba, carrying out the resolution voted at the July foreign ministers' meeting. Many Uruguayans supported the government's action, but Communists were able to organize protests. Even some conservative anti-Communists felt that nonintervention in the political life of any other nation meant that relations could not be broken with a Communist dictatorship. Editorials in most of the newspapers, ranging from traditionally liberal *El Día* to traditionally conservative *El Debate,* pointed out that Cuban subversion in Venezuela constituted the real intervention, not punitive breaks in relations, which sought to discourage attempts at terrorism and insurrection.

A Communist-led group of students occupied a university building in downtown Montevideo, to protest the break with Cuba. The moderate daily *La Mañana* reminded them that their education was tax-supported and open to Uruguayans of all political opinions. Their halting of classes deprived others of an education, including many students who disagreed with their point of view. The students soon went home and the protests stopped. And the chief source of Communist propaganda from any of the diplomatic missions, except for the Soviet Embassy, shut down.

Cuban activities did not cease in 1964 with the closing of the Cuban Embassy in Montevideo. The Uruguayan-Cuban Cultural Institute still functioned, ostensibly to promote understanding of Cuban literature and fine arts among Uruguayan students. After the mid-1967 meeting in Havana of the Organization of Latin American Solidarity (OLAS), this binational institute doubled its activities.

Far more attractive to some Uruguayans of radical inclination have been the publications available at the Uruguayan–East German Cultural Association, such as the magazine *Puente,* which means "Bridge." The theme of such publications and the conferences that the East German group sponsors stress peaceful coexistence between Eastern and Western nations. The moderate image projected prompted several prominent non-Communist Uruguayans to participate in conferences and briefly lured Luis Hierro

Gambardella, minister of culture in the Gestido and Pacheco administrations, onto the binational board of the East German association. Hierro and a few other prominent non-Communist Uruguayan citizens hoped to encourage a reduction in the cold war through more trade and cultural relations between Eastern and Western Europe and between Latin America and Eastern Europe.

The Uruguayan-Cuban Cultural Institute in 1967 made available to the Uruguayan-Chinese Cultural Institute hundreds of copies of Ernesto "Ché" Guevara's book on guerrilla warfare *Guerra de Guerrillas*. After Guevara was killed fighting in Bolivia on October 8, 1967, the Cuban center began to play down the book, whereas the Chinese center promoted it with the same furor shown before Guevara's death. By 1968 the Cuban institute was again pushing this book, whereas the Soviet Union's institute was ignoring it completely.

One Montevideo radio station, CX 30, Radio Nacional, which despite its name is privately owned and a commercial outlet, has been receptive to selling air time to Cuban and Eastern European groups, whereas most Montevideo stations have not. Some of the CX 30 programs cannot be classified as political propaganda, such as those from Prague promoting East-West trade relations. Those paid for by the Uruguayan-Cuban Cultural Institute, however, are billed as cultural broadcasts, but often contain polemic commentaries against the United States, the OAS, business interests in Uruguay, and various moderate non-Communist governments of Latin America. The phraseology always contains enough references to literature and new books to be classified as "literary."

X

A Summary: Somehow It All Works

Winston Churchill once said that democracy was the worst form of government, except for all the other forms that had been tried. Uruguay, with its continuing economic crisis of the 1960's, suffering numerous strikes and uncomfortable inflation, might seem a poor prospect for praise as a leading nation of Latin America. Paraphrasing Churchill, we might say that Uruguay seems to be the worst Latin American nation, except for almost all the others.

This republic during this century contrasts sharply with most other Latin American nations in that, despite economic pressures, Uruguay has not given up its broad-based democracy and genuinely represesentative government. With Communist leaders in labor unions exploiting Latin America's most open society and despite a tradition of welfare benefits for all citizens—even beyond the nation's means to pay for such programs—Uruguay does reflect a negative image. Yet Uruguayans remain politically free, highly literate, and markedly articulate on public issues at home and abroad.

With a hundred voices spouting solutions for problems, all talking at once like a chorus in an Italian opera, public dialogue in Uruguay may seem to be reflecting a nation in bewilderment. Yet one can balance the democratic institutions against the economic pressures and say of Uruguay, "Somehow it all seems to work."

NATIONAL LEADERS

Despite the continuing pressures of inflation and labor unrest, various Uruguayan men in public life continue to offer their services whenever and wherever needed, even though more lucrative and tranquil positions in private life await their return from public service. For example, consider Carlos Manini Ríos, a newspaper publisher who prefers running the daily *La Mañana* to occupying a public post. Since June, 1967, however, he has accepted five exacting appointments.

At that time, Manini Ríos responded to the call of President Gestido to become minister of culture, to direct public education and fine-arts activities at a time of budgetary austerity. Four months later, in October, 1967, Manini Ríos served the administration during a cabinet crisis as acting minister of finance, and then as undersecretary of finance. Then, in December, 1967, when Jorge Pacheco succeeded the late Oscar Gestido as president, Manini Ríos agreed to become director of planning and the budget. In 1968, he moved over to the job of president of the Bank of the Republic.

Deputy Francisco A. Forteza, as chairman of the Finance Committee of the Chamber of Representatives, steered the Emergency Law on appropriations into final form in mid-1967. Then, in December, 1967, he consented to leave the legislative post that had drawn up these difficult guidelines for the executive branch to follow, in order to step into the exacting job of trying to carry them out. He became undersecretary of finance, trying to practice what he had been preaching.

César Charlone, a leading economist, as minister of finance, and Enrique Iglesias, another prominent economist, as director of the Central Bank, in January, 1968, worked out an economic development program to rebuild the nation's reserves. Most Uruguayan leaders, whether oriented to the liberal or the conservative wing of the political spectrum, and whether employed in the public or the private sector of the economy, have sought ways to end inflation through austerity programs that will not negate Uruguay's traditional national concern for those citizens with the lowest incomes. The dilemma remains: to wage war on poverty and inflation at the same time.

No nation can do everything at once. As former French Premier Pierre Mendès-France once said, "To govern is to choose." In the United States in the late 1960's, the great debates over public policies involved financing exploration of space, eradicating city slums, and funding programs to lessen poverty, at a time when the nation was enmeshed in costly military action in Vietnam. In Uruguay, during the same period of time, the debates focused on continued welfare programs in the face of lower world prices for wool, as numerous strikes for pay increases continued to push inflation upward.

Statistical Perspective

As economists with the international finance division of the U.S. Federal Reserve System have pointed out, Uruguay's GNP has not grown in terms of dollars or purchasing power in more than a decade. In 1955, the GNP totaled 4.59 billion pesos, and by 1963 that figure was 22.47 billion pesos. But, for any meaningful comparison, both figures should be expressed in the value of 1955 pesos, to avoid the confusion that continuing loss in value of the peso has meant. Thus, in 1955 pesos, the Uruguayan GNP for 1963 was 4.96 billion pesos, almost equal to the 1955 GNP. Similarly, the 1967 GNP approximated the 1955 GNP.

Without using pesos, we can analyze the relative emphasis that the government places on various segments of Uruguayan public affairs by considering the percentages that the major government categories received in the 1967 budget.

Branch	Percentage
Executive *(presidency, cabinet, agencies)*	32.7
Judicial system *(all courts)*	1.1
General Assembly *(includes professional staffs)*	2.9

Branch	Percentage
Public education *(primary, secondary, higher)*	26.9
General services *(includes welfare services)*	30.6
Decentralized entities *(public corporations)*	5.4
Miscellaneous	0.4
Total	100.0

We can see that Uruguay devotes much of its public funds to its schools and to welfare benefits for citizens of all ages. The budget thus reflects the emphasis of the chapters, above, on education and the economy. Relatively small amounts of money go into developmental investments, explaining in part the stagnation of the Uruguayan economy in terms of genuine growth in goods and services.

Uruguay has chosen to emphasize consumption more than production, and public policies of recent decades reflect this inclination. In 1950, Uruguayan prosperity rested on a solid foundation of cattle and wool production. By 1968, this same nation was suffering, as are other nations in the world that live beyond their means and rely on foreign borrowing more than on expansion of their own economic base.

Throughout the 1960's, the public and private sectors have been caught in a spiral of inflation. Factional struggles among various special-interest groups to secure for themselves greater portions of the national income raged against a backdrop of numerous strikes, which reduced anticipated private and public earnings. Until the 1960's, Uruguay enjoyed a rate of saving that economists considered adequate for national economic health. But surplus capital has not been invested in ways that would produce more new payrolls and higher production in established industries. In 1968, unemployment reached 12 per cent of the potential adult work force.

Given Uruguay's twentieth-century history of progressive, democratic government, the adoption of severe executive decrees to meet the economic crisis and social tensions has not been easy for President Pacheco, politically or personally. On June 24, 1968, when he ordered army troops to bolster police guarding banks to ensure no interruption in service by a Communist-led group trying to intimidate bank employees, he explained the situation carefully to the nation. And most citizens seemed to understand, for leaders of rival factions of the Colorado and Blanco parties stepped forward to support Pacheco's stand.

Deputy Juan Pablo Terra, leader of the Christian Democratic Party in the General Assembly, called for a popular front to restore unity in the republic. Colorado and Blanco leaders answered that the traditional political system of Uruguay already possessed the kind of governmental structure and political-party coexistence needed for unity. By 1969, Uruguay was recovering from inflation, thanks to the freeze on wages and prices. In 1967, the cost of living rose by 136 per cent; in 1968, by 66 per cent; and, for 1969, it was estimated that it would increase by only 20–30 per cent.

The 1970's will test Uruguay as the Banda Oriental has never been tested before. Can a nation that exerted every effort for civil liberties and welfare benefits evoke a consensus that will stop fomenters of work stoppages from sabotaging economic growth? The age-old question remains: can an open society remain so when some elements within it abuse their right to dissent by efforts to destroy the nation? The question echoed in Europe and North America. Uruguay has been a social laboratory, an inspiration to other Latin American nations seeking political freedom. Now Uruguay's own economic life has been threatened, as has, by implication, the broad-based democracy of the republic.

Since the turn of the century, the spirit of Batlle has engendered a touch of greatness in the Uruguayan people. In time of trouble—from the economic depression of the 1930's, through the wartime exigencies of the 1940's, to the subtle pressures of the cold war of the 1950's—citizens of the Banda Oriental have faced up to their problems. In the 1960's, the Uruguayans searched for a political solution to inefficiencies in public life, ending the experiment with a plural presidency in favor of a return to a vigorous chief executive. But the heart of Uruguayan troubles—

overspending of the nation's earnings and unlimited tolerance of demagogic work stoppages in the face of ruinous inflation—has not been confronted.

Realistic politicians have been saying that no combination of government officials and political parties can reduce very much the number of people on public payrolls. Rather, the private sector of the economy must be expanded while the public sector is kept at its current level. Whatever the formulas implemented, Uruguay cannot fail much longer to confront the spiral of inflation, halt it, and reduce it. Marxist and other political extremists seek chaos, for Uruguayan democracy stands as a reminder to all Latin America that traditional representative government can speak for all the citizens of a nation. Somehow, Uruguayan leaders continue to try to do just that. Such a goal is ancient, timeless, but for much of this century it has been part of the destiny of Uruguay.

Bibliography

GOVERNMENT PUBLICATIONS

Pan American Union, Department of Legal Affairs. *A Statement of the Laws of Uruguay in Matters Affecting Business.* 4th ed. Washington, D.C.: Organization of American States, 1963.

Uruguay, Camara de Representantes, Comisión de Hacienda. *Ley de Emergencia,* XL Legislatura, July 14, 1967, 46 pp. This emergency law was invoked by the President of Uruguay in June, 1968, to set price and wage ceilings to combat inflation.

Uruguay, *El Diario* Official Staff (eds.). *Registro nacional de leyes y decretos de la república.* Annual volume, which gives the laws enacted by the national legislature.

BOOKS AND ARTICLES

General

FITZGIBBON, RUSSELL H. *Uruguay: Portrait of a Democracy.* New Brunswick, N.J.: Rutgers University Press, 1954. This classic study of Uruguayan politics, economics, and social life has been reprinted by Russell and Russell (New York, 1966).

PENDLE, GEORGE. *Uruguay.* 3d ed. New York: Oxford University Press, 1965. A brief overview of the culture, politics, and economics of Uruguay.

TAYLOR, PHILIP B., JR. *Government and Politics of Uruguay.* New Orleans: Tulane University Studies in Political Science, 1960. Government, politics, economics, and general culture are covered.

History

ACEVEDO, EDUARDO. *Historia uruguaya: Después de Artigas.* 3d ed. Montevideo: Monteverde, 1943. Acevedo's history is still available in reprint form in Montevideo bookstores.

BENVENUTO, LUIS CARLOS. *Breve historia del Uruguay.* Montevideo: Arca, 1967. This compact history goes through the 1967 restoration of the office of the presidency.

HUDSON, W. H. *The Purple Land.* New York: E. P. Dutton & Co., 1927; London: J. M. Dent & Sons, 1951. This reprint of the 1885 original describes nineteenth-century gaucho life.

PIVEL DEVOTO, JUAN E. and ALCIRA. *Historia de la república oriental del Uruguay (1830–1930).* Montevideo: Editorial Medina, 1945. The most widely consulted history in Uruguay.

STREET, JOHN. *Artigas and the Emancipation of Uruguay.* New York: Cambridge University Press, 1959. In 1967 the Institute of Historical Studies of the University of the Republic in Montevideo published a Spanish translation of this history.

VANGER, MILTON I. *José Batlle y Ordóñez of Uruguay: The Creator of His Times, 1902–1907.* Cambridge, Mass.: Harvard University Press, 1963.

ZUM FELDE, ALBERTO. *Proceso histórico del Uruguay.* 5th ed. Montevideo: Arca, 1967. The largest-selling history in Uruguay.

Government and Politics

ALISKY, MARVIN. "Uruguay," in Martin C. Needler (ed.), *Political Systems of Latin America.* 2d ed. Princeton: D. Van Nostrand Co., 1969.

BRAY, DONALD W. "Uruguay," in Ben G. Burnett and Kenneth F. Johnson (eds.), *Political Forces in Latin America.* Belmont, Calif.: Wadsworth Publishing Co., 1968.

GROS ESPIELL, HECTOR. *La corte electoral.* Montevideo: Facultad de Derecho, Universidad de la República, 1960. This law-school text explains the machinery of elections.

Institute for the Comparative Study of Political Systems. *Uruguay Election Factbook, November 27, 1966.* Washington, D.C.: Operations and Policy Research, 1966. Editor Henry Wells summarizes many data about elected officials.

JIMENEZ DE ARÉCHAGA, JUSTINO. *La constitución de 1952.* 4 vols. Montevideo: Medina, 1952. A leading legal scholar explains Uruguayan constitutional law.

LINDAHL, GORAN G. *Uruguay's New Path: A Study of Politics During the First Colegiado, 1919–33.* Stockholm: Institute of Ibero-American Studies of Sweden, 1962.

ROVIRA, ALEJANDRO. *La constitución uruguaya de 1966.* Montevideo: Editorial Diálogo, 1967. An analysis of the 1966 constitution.

Economics

Asociación de Bancos del Uruguay. *Información económica.* A monthly bulletin of the Uruguayan Bank Association, issued in Montevideo.

BAKLANOFF, ERIC N. "Notes on the Pathology of Uruguay's Welfare

State," *Mississippi Valley Journal of Business and Economics* (April, 1967), pp. 63–69.

BRANNON, RUSSELL H. *The Agricultural Development of Uruguay.* New York: Frederick A. Praeger, 1968.

DALY, HERMAN E. "The Uruguayan Economy: Its Basic Nature and Current Problems" *Journal of Inter-American Relations* (July, 1965), pp. 316–30.

HANSON, SIMON G. *Utopia in Uruguay.* New York: Oxford University Press, 1938. The classic reference on the Uruguayan economy.

IGLESIAS, ENRIQUE. *Uruguay: Una propuesta de combio.* Montevideo: Alfa, 1966. Every major proposal in this book has been the subject of congressional debate during 1967 and 1968.

MARTÍNEZ LAMAS, JULIO. *Riqueza y pobreza del Uruguay.* Montevideo: Atlántida, 1946. This book has been quoted more by government and business leaders of Uruguay than has any other work on economics dealing with the republic.

REDDING, DAVID C. "The Economic Decline of Uruguay," *Inter-American Economic Affairs* (Spring, 1967), pp. 55–72.

Legal Literature

CLAGETT, HELEN L. *A Guide to the Law and Legal Literature of Uruguay.* Washington, D.C.: Library of Congress, 1947.

EDER, PHANOR J. *A Comparative Survey of Anglo-American and Latin-American Law.* New York: New York University Press, 1950.

Culture

ALISKY, MARVIN. "Uruguay Prizes Its Print, Broadcast Press," *The Quill* (October, 1967), pp. 32–34.

American International Association. *La prensa del interior del Uruguay.* Montevideo: Asociación Internacional Americana, 1966. A detailed description of the newspapers of the small towns and departmental capitals of Uruguay.

ARDAO, ARTURO. *La filosofía en el Uruguay en el siglo XX.* México, D.F.: Fondo de Cultura Económica, 1956. A discussion of the Uruguayan philosophers of the twentieth century.

CRAWFORD, W. REX. *A Century of Latin-American Thought.* Rev. ed. New York: Frederick A. Praeger, 1966. Uruguay's most influential thinkers are compared with other Latin American philosophers.

DUARTE, JACINTO A. *Dos siglos de publicidad en la historia del Uruguay.* Montevideo: Editorial Sur, 1952. Early periodicals of Uruguay are related to their times.

FIGUEIRA, GASTON. "Interpretación del Uruguay," *Journal of Inter-American Studies* (October, 1967), pp. 483–87.

HADDOX, JOHN H. "Carlos Vaz Ferreira: Uruguayan Philosopher," *Journal of Inter-American Studies* (October, 1966), pp. 595–600.

LUISI, LUISA. "Two Great Uruguayan Writers," in *Literature in Latin America*. Washington, D.C.: Pan American Union, 1950.

MAGGI, CARLOS. *El Uruguay y su gente*. Montevideo: Alfa, 1965. Uruguay's leading playwright and essayist philosophizes that the small republic has benefited from political moderation but lacks the exotic unintegrated minorities to attract tourists away from its beaches.

SOLARI, ALDO E. *Estudios sobre la sociedad uruguaya*. 2 vols. Montevideo: Arca, 1964 and 1965. Uruguay's leading sociologist analyzes the middle-class society of the republic.

———— and LIPSET, SEYMOUR MARTIN (eds.). *Elites in Latin America*. New York: Oxford University Press, 1967. The political-economic-social elite of Uruguay has shown a more democratic inclination than has its counterparts in most other Latin American nations.

TINKER, EDWIN L. *The Horsemen of the Americas*. Rev: ed. Austin: University of Texas Press, 1967. The gauchos of Uruguay, Argentina, and Brazil are described in detail before modern farm and ranch machinery changed their life on the pampa.

ZUM FELDE, ALBERTO. *Proceso intelectual del Uruguay*. Buenos Aires: Editorial Claridad, 1941. A historical analysis of the great thinkers of Uruguay.

Index

172   INDEX